W9-APS-153

THE SMALL BOAT CERTIFICATION SERIES

Learn Sailing Right!

INTERMEDIATE SAILING

Dedicated to Glenn Lattimore

The National Standard for Quality Sailing Instruction

Published by the UNITED STATES SAILING ASSOCIATION Copyright © 2015 by the UNITED STATES SAILING ASSOCIATION.
All rights reserved. No part of this publication may be reproduced, stored in a retrieval system, or transmitted, in any form or by any means, electronic, mechanical, photocopying, recording, or otherwise without prior written permission from the UNITED STATES SAILING ASSOCIATION.
Printed in the United States of America.
UNITED STATES SAILING ASSOCIATION P.O. Box 1260, 15 Maritime Drive, Portsmouth, RI 02871-0907
ISBN 978-0-9821676-8-7.

www.ussailing.org
www.sailingcertification.com

Cover Image: Onne van der Wal

ACKNOWLEDGMENTS

Emlie Barkow hails from Pine Lake, WI amongst a large family of sailors. Emlie graduated from Hobart & William Smith Colleges where she sailed and received her teaching certification. Emlie has been Program Director at Pleon Yacht Club, in Marblehead MA and Newport Harbor Yacht Club in Newport, CA, before her current position of Sailing Director at Lido Isle Yacht Club, CA.

Morgan Collins Is the past chair of the Community Sailing Council. Morgan is a Level 1 and 2 Instructor Trainer, a US Powerboating instructor, a member of small boat national faculty and a former recipient of the "Marty Luray Award" which is presented annually to the person who has made an outstanding and unselfish contribution to furthering public access to sailing.

Guy Fleming has been working for Waikiki Yacht Club since 1985 and has been their Sailing Director since 1991. He was certified as a Level 1 IT and Level 2 CT in 1993 before becoming a Master Instructor Trainer in 1995. Since then he has been certified as a Regional Race Officer, a US Sailing Judge, a Powerboat Instructor, a Basic Keelboat Instructor Trainer and a Level 3 coach. When not teaching or coaching sailing, Guy enjoys his time on the water, competing in Lasers, kitesurfing or stand-up paddling.

Stu Gilfillen is the Training Director at US Sailing. He previously served as the Executive Director of the Sarasota Youth Sailing Program in Sarasota, FL and Sailing Director for both the Edgartown and Beverly Yacht Clubs. Currently the staff liaison to US Sailing's Community Sailing Council and Commercial Sailing Schools, he is a US Sailing Level 1 Instructor Trainer, a Level 2 coach and a US Powerboating Instructor. Stu also serves as the organizer for US Sailing's National Sailing Programs Symposium.

Kim Hapgood has served as the Program Director for Sail Newport since 1996. She's a member of the US Sailing Training Committee, co-chair of small boat National Faculty, a Master Instructor Trainer, avid match racer and semi-active judge. She completed her undergraduate work at Brandeis University and her graduate degree in Higher Education Administration at Columbia University. Additionally, she's a seasonal part-time Harbormaster for City of Newport, RI.

Hart Kelley is the Head Sail Training Coach for cadet leadership training in the Coastal Sail Training Program at the US Coast Guard Academy. He is co-chair of the Small Boat National Faculty, Vice-Chair of Standards and Credentials for the Training Committee, a Level 1 Master Instructor Trainer, Level 2 Coach Trainer, Basic Keelboat Instructor Trainer, Keelboat Cruising Instructor Trainer, Powerboat Instructor and frequent speaker at the National Sailing Programs Symposium.

Steve Maddox serves as a US Sailing Small Boat Instructor Trainer and Coach Trainer and US Powerboating Master Instructor Trainer, and as a regional training coordinator for both. He also is the founder and president of SeaAffinity, Inc., a non-profit sailing program in Baltimore, MD.

Rachael Miller is the founder/Director of the Rozalia Project for a Clean Ocean whose mission is to find and remove marine debris using remotely operated vehicles, sonar, and nets from aboard American Promise, a Ted Hood 60'. She is a member of the US Sailing National Faculty and Training Committee as well as a Level 1 and 2 Instructor Trainer. Rachael raced Lasers, Europe Dinghies, J24s and was a member of the Brown University Sailing Team. She is a certified windsurfing, kitesurfing and snowkiting instructor.

Deb Sullivan-Gravelle grew up in Boulder, Colorado. After college she moved to Seattle, Washington where she was introduced to sailing and never looked back. One of the co-founders of Sail Sand Point in Seattle, Deb spent 4 years running the Bermuda Sailing Association before returning to Colorado. She is a Level 1 Instructor Trainer and Level 2 Coach Trainer a member of the National Faculty and is a former organizer of the National Sailing Programs Symposium.

Joe Comeau loves to draw and has been creating illustrations for a variety of projects for over 10 years. He grew up on Narragansett Bay and honed his craft drawing parts of his family's 25 foot Coronado, when he wasn't stowing sails or trying to keep his sketchbook dry that is.

TABLE OF CONTENTS

Introduction. 4

Chapter 1:
Preparing Yourself for Sailing. 6
Cold and Heat Emergencies 6
Proper Gear 6
Hydration. 7
Ditty Bag 7

Chapter 2:
Wind, Weather, Tides and Currents. 8
Reading Wind on the Water 8
Wind Velocity 8
Lifts and Headers. 9
True and Apparent Wind 10
Weather. 11
Tides and Currents 14

Chapter 3:
Sail Shape and Controls. 16
General Rules for Sail Controls 16
Assessing Sail Shape 16
Using Sail Controls for Upwind Sailing . . . 17
Using Sail Controls for Downwind Sailing. 21

Chapter 4:
How Sailing Works 22
The Science of Sailing. 22
How a Sail Works. 22
How a Foil Works. 23
Balance: Sails and Foils Work Together . . 24
Weather Helm. 25
Lee Helm 25

Chapter 5:
Body Position 26
Side-to-Side Position for Upwind 26
Side-to-Side Position for Downwind 27
Fore and Aft Position, Upwind 28
Fore and Aft Position, Downwind. 28
Hiking Techniques 29
Holding the Tiller Extension & Mainsheet . 30
Handling Lines 30

Chapter 6:
Close Hauled and Upwind Sailing 31
Refining Upwind Sailing 31
Roll Tacking 33

Chapter 7:
Jibing Techniques and Downwind Sailing. . 34
Speed Is Your Friend. 34
Methods for Quicker Sail Transition. 34
Steering Jibes 35
Roll Jibing. 36
Avoiding Capsizes to Windward. 38

Chapter 8:
Rigging and Seamanship. 40
Knots. 40
Paddling and Sculling 41
Shortening Sail. 42
Docking. 43
Anchoring. 44
Towing. 45

Chapter 9:
Emergency Procedures 46
Capsizing 46
Heaving-To. 49
Running Aground. 49
Signaling Distress 50
Overboard Rescue. 50

Chapter 10:
Navigation & Rules of the Road 53
Navigation. 53
Navigation Aids 53
Rules of the Road. 54

Chapter 11:
Maintenance. 57
Pre-Sail 57
Post-Sail 59
Storm Preparations. 59

Introduction

Learn Sailing Right! Intermediate Sailing is about sailing faster and smarter with greater confidence. As an intermediate sailor, you no longer need to think about how to tack, return to the dock or rig your boat. These maneuvers are now as natural as breathing to you. It will start to become apparent to you that rigging a boat, tacking, and returning to the dock are not separate skills, but everything is interrelated. Where sailing is simplified for beginners as they learn fundamental skills and concepts, intermediate sailors are ready for deeper explanations and some of the details behind how a sailboat works.

As an intermediate sailor, you will use the science of how a boat moves and how sails function to improve your boat performance. You will learn and practice more complex maneuvers, develop new skills and learn how to use new sail controls. As an intermediate sailor you can expect longer sessions out sailing as you perfect your skills and maneuvers.

The first section of Learn Sailing Right! Intermediate Sailing introduces sailors to concepts and theories on how a sailboat works. In the first chapters—Preparing Yourself for Sailing (chapter 1), Wind, Weather, Tides and Currents (chapter 2), Sail Shape and Controls (chapter 3), How Sailing Works (chapter 4), and Body Position and Boat Balance (chapter 5)—you will learn the reasons why a sailboat moves and how to make it move more efficiently.

In the next section, you will be introduced to more advanced boathandling skills and rigging techniques as you implement the concepts and theories introduced in the first section of the book.

These chapters include Close Hauled and Upwind Sailing (chapter 6) and Jibing Techniques and Downwind Sailing (chapter 7), which cover techniques and skills for improved upwind and downwind sailing.

Finally, the remaining chapters will teach intermediate sailors about safety, seamanship and self-rescuing skills in Rigging and Seamanship chapter 8),

(Emergency Procedures (chapter 9),
Navigation & Rules of the Road (chapter 10),
and Maintenance (chapter 11).

Mastering the skills covered in this book
prepares you for a number of different
paths to advanced sailing. For those with a
competitive spirit, racing sailboats may be
your preference.

Perhaps day cruising and navigation suit
you better, or what really interests you
is a chance to zoom around on a high-
performance skiff. Regardless of which
pursuit appeals to you—or even if you are
interested in all types of sailing—this book
will prepare you for your chosen course.

CHAPTER 1

PREPARING YOURSELF FOR SAILING

► Cold and Heat Emergencies
► Proper Gear
► Hydration
► Ditty Bag

With longer stretches of time spent out on the water, you need to consider what additional items will make your sailing experience safe and fun. Before you launch and set sail do not forget to prepare yourself for success on the water.

COLD AND HEAT EMERGENCIES
Exposure to the elements can drain you of energy and sap your concentration. When that exposure is extreme, it can even threaten your health and well-being. Keep an eye out for odd behavior in yourself and others. Sluggishness, confusion, yawning and shivering are all symptoms of *hypothermia*. Hypothermia, the lowering of your core body temperature, can happen in the middle of summer as well as in the cooler months of the year. Make sure someone with symptoms of hypothermia is moved to a dry, warm environment and allowed to warm up.

Heat emergencies such as heat exhaustion and heat stroke can be life threatening. In both situations treatment is to cool the person down. Anyone suffering a heat emergency should be removed to a cooler environment; medical attention should be provided in severe cases.

PROPER GEAR
Most cold and heat emergencies are preventable with proper gear. Keeping dry despite windborne spray and water is highly advisable. Foul-weather gear, hats, boots or sailing shoes, and protective attire such as rash guards can help protect you from both heat and cold exposure. Layering and appropriate gear for the conditions is the correct course of action to prevent heat emergencies. If you are unsure what gear you should have, ask a sailing instructor or an experienced sailor in your area.

TIP

► Remember when thinking about gear that water temperature is as much a concern as air temperature. In the spring, warm air can fool a sailor into dressing lightly. However, the cool water temperature will be a quick reminder to use layers to protect yourself!

HYDRATION

Stay hydrated by drinking plenty of water or sport drinks. Staying hydrated helps to fend off many heat emergencies and keeps you functioning at a high level. Through perspiration you will lose a lot of fluid while you are out on the water, so be sure to bring something to drink. Water is the best choice.

DITTY BAG

A sailor keeps tools, a knife, spare parts, a whistle, extra line and other useful parts, pieces and safety devices in a small pouch called a *ditty bag*. Since you may be out on the water for longer stretches, having the resources to repair small problems will keep you sailing. Instructors will often carry these items for their sailing class, but if you are without that type of support, bring your own ditty bag.

Photo: Steve Maddox

CHAPTER 2

WIND, WEATHER, TIDES AND CURRENTS

▶ Reading Wind on the Water
▶ Wind Velocity
▶ Lifts and Headers
▶ True and Apparent Wind
▶ Weather
▶ Tides and Currents

In beginning sailing you learned how to sail upwind and downwind, tack, jibe and reach. All of that was in the context of a single, unwavering wind direction. Once out on the water you noticed that the wind actually changes in both velocity and direction. Learning how to anticipate those changes allows you to become a better sailor. You will sail faster, make better sail adjustments, improve the course you are sailing, enjoy sailing more and maybe even impress your friends! The following chapter identifies a variety of methods for anticipating changes in the wind, weather, tides and currents.

READING WIND ON THE WATER

Reading wind on the water is somewhat like looking into the future. Since ripples and waves are a function of wind, understanding how the wind causes waves and ripples clues you in to both wind direction and velocity.

Wind has friction with the surface of the water, which creates waves and ripples; the stronger the wind, the bigger the waves and ripples. With practice you can determine the true wind direction, as well as see increases and decreases in wind speed. Water reading gives a sailor data on a short-term basis. It is not difficult to realize the advantage of knowing whether the wind ahead is going to change in velocity or direction.

WIND VELOCITY

Wind velocity is the speed of the wind. Generally, this is measured in either miles per hour (mph) or nautical miles per hour (knots). The velocity of wind is constantly changing. We call patches of decreased velocity a ***lull*** and increased velocity a ***puff***. You can determine lulls and puffs by looking at the various colors and textures of the water. The water's surface will have more pronounced ripples and darker colors in the puffs, and less pronounced ripples and lighter colors in lulls. Learning to anticipate these changes in wind velocity is important to promote boat speed through sail trim, boat heel and boat handling.

TIP

▶ You can practice reading wind on the water by standing on a fixed dock or stationary boat while you watch puffs travel across the water's surface.

▶ Remember these useful equations:
1 knot = 1.1 MPH
10 knots = 11 MPH

WIND SPEED (KNOTS) SEA AND SAILING CONDITIONS

WIND SPEED (KNOTS)	SEA AND SAILING CONDITIONS
0-10	**LIGHT WIND** Smooth water with small waves. The boat will be easy to handle under full sail.
11-16	**MEDIUM WIND** Moderate seas with some white caps. If the boat feels overpowered, consider reefing one of the sails for a more comfortable ride.
17-21	**HEAVY WIND** Lengthening waves with many white caps and some spray. Boat will become more difficult to manage and you should seriously consider reefing.
22-27	**VERY HEAVY WIND** Large waves, many white caps and spray. Boat will need at least one reef in the mainsail and a smaller jib. These conditions require considerable sailing experience. Listen to radio weather reports for small craft advisories.
28-47	**SEVERE WIND** Gale conditions. High waves with white caps and foaming waves. This is a good time to stay ashore!

TIP

▶ A header on one tack is a lift on the opposite tack.

▶ A wind that consistently shifts in a clockwise direction is said to be a veering or clocking wind.

▶ A wind that consistently shifts in a counterclockwise direction is said to be backing.

LIFTS AND HEADERS

In the same way that the speed of the wind is never constant, the direction that the wind is coming from is also constantly changing or shifting. *Wind shifts* range from almost unnoticeable to major swings in direction. Wind shifts will play a major role in how you sail since they will affect the course that you are able to sail.

A lift is when the wind's direction shifts from the bow toward the stern. A header is a wind shift toward the bow. Lifts or headers will require an adjustment to the course you are sailing, or an adjustment to your sail trim.

TRUE AND APPARENT WIND

When it comes to knowing about the wind the most common source of information is a weather station. Meteorological weather stations are always stationary, which allows them to record accurate readings of the *true wind* direction and velocity. But, what would happen if the weather station were attached to a moving object, such as a boat or a car? The motion of the weather station would change the wind readings, depending on the direction and speed the weather station is moving. The altered wind direction and velocity, which is different from the true wind direction because of the motion of the weather station, is known as *apparent wind*.

Since boats are moving objects they always sail in apparent wind. Trim your sails or adjust your course by using the telltales on the sails. Changes in a boat's course or speed as well as puffs, lulls, lifts and headers will all affect a boat's apparent wind and require sail trim adjustments or course adjustments. Keep the windward and leeward telltales streaming to maximize your sail trim.

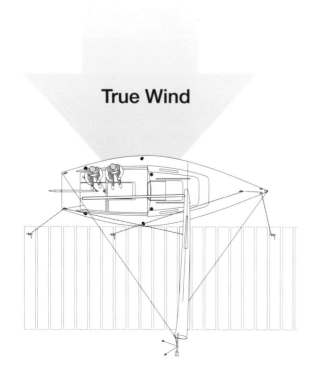

True Wind

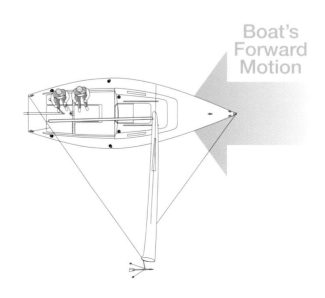

Boat's Forward Motion

WEATHER

One of the general safety checks you should make before going out sailing is becoming aware of the weather all around you. Some good sources for weather information include:

▶ NOAA (many boats have VHF radios with a special station for weather)
▶ Your local radio and TV stations
▶ Websites
▶ Airline pilot weather guides (available online)
▶ Newspapers
▶ Your own weather station with a thermometer, barometer and hydrometer

Weather constantly changes, so learning how to predict the weather based on your observations will keep you focused on sailing in the safest possible conditions. Clues to impending weather include changes in wind direction, cloud patterns and falling temperatures. It is also helpful to keep your eye on the sky—both prior to sailing and while you are out on the water. The following chart will help you learn more about your own sky observations and predicted weather activity.

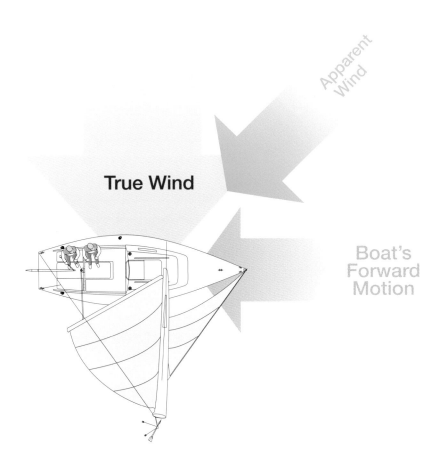

Apparent Wind

True Wind

Boat's Forward Motion

CHAPTER 2

Cumulus clouds, which are large, white, and fluffy, are often an indicator of good weather.

Wispy, thin **cirrus clouds** usually mean good weather for the day, but may be a prediction that a change in weather is on the way.

Towering **cumulonimbus clouds**, or "thunderheads" are usually accompanied by severe conditions, including heavy rain and lightning.

Low layered **stratus clouds** usually bring steady rain.

OBSERVATION	PREDICTION
Sun and clear sky in the morning	Onshore winds during the day; offshore winds (land breezes) during the night, usually dying in the early morning
Calm, overcast days	Continued calm and overcast, unless the sun comes out
Cold and warm fronts	Showers or rain, changing air temperature, winds shifting in a clockwise direction (cold fronts usually move faster than warm fronts)
High cirrus clouds	Warm front with rain and changing winds should appear in a couple of days; clouds will get lower and denser as the front gets closer.
Cumulus clouds growing taller (cumulonimbus)	Thunderstorms and strong winds
Dark clouds approaching	A squall or storm

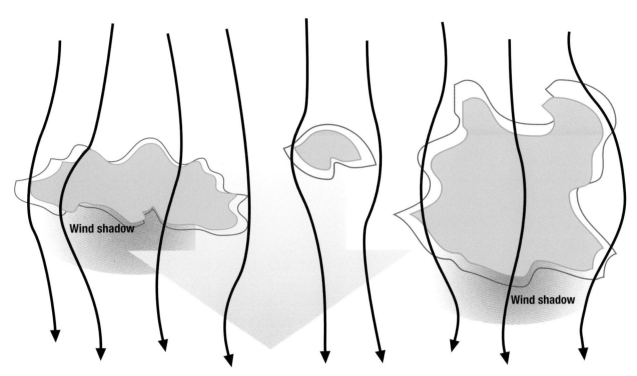

Land Effects

Wind conditions can be affected by nearby land features. Islands, tall buildings, even anchored ships cast *wind shadows* (areas of less wind) on their leeward sides. Sailing from fresh winds into one of these wind shadows greatly depowers a sailboat.

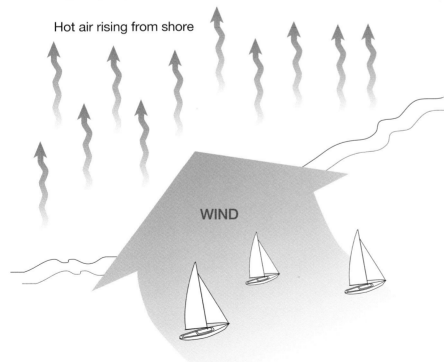

Hot air rising from shore

WIND

Thermal Winds

Local winds are often caused by differences in temperature between the shore and neighboring water. As denser cool air is drawn toward rising warm air, wind is created. These winds are commonly referred to as "onshore breezes" and "sea breezes." The technical term is *thermal wind*. The most famous illustration of thermal wind is on San Francisco Bay, where hot air rising out of the Sacramento Valley, about 75 miles inland from San Francisco, creates a vacuum that draws in 25-knot winds through the Golden Gate almost every summer afternoon like clockwork.

TIDES AND CURRENTS

Tides and currents will have an important influence on just about every aspect of sailing—especially when you are planning a course to sail, avoiding obstructions and docking or landing at a mooring.

A tide table (partially shown, right) gives you daily information regarding the predicted times of high and low tides and the heights of the tides.

NEWPORT, RI

HIGH & LOW WATER   41°30'N   71°20'W

CORRECTED FOR DAYLIGHT SAVING TIME: APRIL 2 – OCTOBER 28

MAY				JUNE				JULY				AUGUST			
Time	ft	Time	ft	Time	ft	Time	ft	Time	ft	Time	ft	Time	ft	Time	ft
1 0306 -0.1 0936 3.5 M 1456 0.0 2153 4.0		**16** 0309 -0.8 0939 4.2 Tu 1513 -0.7 2202 4.9		**1** 0345 0.2 1035 3.3 Th 1543 0.3 2249 3.7		**16** 0439 -0.5 1108 4.2 F 1651 -0.2 2330 4.5		**1** 0357 0.1 1052 3.5 Sa 1603 0.3 2305 3.8		**16** 0502 -0.2 1136 4.3 Su 1726 0.1 2357 4.1		**1** 0447 -0.0 1151 3.9 Tu 1714 0.3		**16** 0014 3.6 0543 0.3 W 1245 3.9 1825 0.8	
2 0335 0.0 1017 3.3 Tu 1530 0.1 2233 3.8		**17** 0401 -0.7 1032 4.1 W 1606 -0.5 2255 4.7		**2** 0420 0.2 1119 3.2 F 1622 0.4 2332 3.5		**17** 0530 -0.3 1203 4.1 Sa 1749 0.1		**2** 0433 0.1 1135 3.5 Su 1646 0.4 2348 3.6		**17** 0546 0.0 1229 4.1 M 1820 0.4		**2** 0008 3.6 0531 0.0 W 1241 3.9 1806 0.4		**17** 0105 3.3 0623 0.6 Th 1338 3.7) 1915 1.0	
3 0407 0.1 1100 3.2 W 1605 0.3 2316 3.5		**18** 0453 -0.6 1127 4.0 Th 1702 -0.3 2351 4.4		**3** 0457 0.3 1205 3.2 Sa 1706 0.5		**18** 0025 4.1 0622 -0.0 Su 1259 4.1 1853 0.3		**3** 0512 0.2 1221 3.5 M 1733 0.5		**18** 0049 3.7 0631 0.3 Tu 1322 3.9 1918 0.7		**3** 0100 3.4 0620 0.1 Th 1337 3.9 (1905 0.5		**18** 0159 3.1 0708 0.8 F 1434 3.5 2019 1.2	
4 0442 0.2 1145 3.0 Th 1645 0.4		**19** 0549 -0.3 1225 3.8 F 1803 0.0		**4** 0017 3.4 0538 0.3 Su 1253 3.2 1755 0.6		**19** 0121 3.8 0716 0.2 M 1356 3.9) 2004 0.6		**4** 0035 3.4 0557 0.2 Tu 1311 3.6 1826 0.5		**19** 0142 3.4 0717 0.5 W 1417 3.8) 2027 0.9		**4** 0200 3.3 0716 0.2 F 1438 4.0 2012 0.5		**19** 0257 2.9 0803 0.9 Sa 1531 3.5 2149 1.2	
5 0000 3.3 0521 0.4 F 1233 2.9 1729 0.5		**20** 0049 4.1 0648 -0.1 Sa 1325 3.8 1913 0.3		**5** 0107 3.2 0625 0.3 M 1345 3.2 1851 0.6		**20** 0218 3.5 0813 0.4 Tu 1453 3.8 2124 0.7		**5** 0127 3.3 0646 0.3 W 1406 3.7 (1926 0.5		**20** 0238 3.2 0808 0.7 Th 1513 3.7 2149 1.0		**5** 0304 3.3 0821 0.2 Sa 1540 4.2 2127 0.5		**20** 0355 2.9 0908 1.0 Su 1625 3.5 2303 1.1	

RHODE ISLAND

These photos, taken at the same location, show the difference between high and low tide. Consulting a tide table and a chart will help you avoid running aground during a low tide.

Tides are defined as the **vertical** movement of water caused by the gravitational pull of the Earth and the Moon. We describe tides as being *high* or *low*, and they occur daily and at regular intervals. On the U.S. East Coast and West Coast, there are typically two high and two low tides each day, but the difference in water height can vary depending on location. A tide that is going out or dropping is said to be **ebbing**, while an incoming tide is *flooding*. The period in between, with very little water movement, is known as **slack**. With a watch, a tide table and a chart, you can determine the depth of the water in which you are sailing at any time. Most freshwater lakes do not have tides.

Current is the **horizontal** flow of water and is described in terms of the direction and speed the water is moving. Current can be caused either by water flowing from a higher elevation to a lower elevation like a river, or by ocean tides going out (ebbing) and coming in (flooding).

Current is affected by water depth. Deep water will increase the speed of current or tide; shallow water will reduce the velocity of current. It is important to know the direction and speed of current when you are sailing. Looking at certain indicators—such as a floating object, a fixed mooring, channel marker or docks—are good ways to determine current. Current flowing past these objects can create a swirl or "wake" that moves in the direction of the current, making the stationary object appear as if it were moving.

When you are sailing against or abeam of a strong current, you may need to compensate by steering upstream and heading higher than your destination. Due to your adjusted heading, your progress toward a destination will be slower, even though the boat appears to be moving at a normal speed. This is the result of the water moving underneath the boat, much like walking up the wrong way on an escalator. If you are unable to sail against the current, the best solution is to anchor the boat and wait for the wind to increase, for the current to change direction, or for a tow.

This buoy is being carried by the current. You can see that it is leaning in the direction of the current, and the moving water is leaving a wake as it passes the buoy.

Compensating for Current

If you are going to sail across a current you can compensate for the effect it will have on your boat. Instead of steering directly toward your goal, steer for a point upstream, and let the current pull you back to your desired course.

WIND

non-adjusted heading

actual path

adjusted heading

actual path

Non-Adjusted Heading

This boat aimed directly for destination ⊗ but was pulled downstream by the current.

CURRENT

Adjusted Heading

This boat steered a course upstream of ⊗ and reached its destination as planned.

CHAPTER 3

SAIL SHAPE AND CONTROLS

▶ General Rules for Sail Controls
▶ Assessing Sail Shape
▶ Using Sail Controls for Upwind Sailing
▶ Using Sail Controls for Downwind Sailing

The shape of a sail directly impacts how well the sail works and how fast the boat will move. Sail controls are used to adjust a sail's shape by powering and depowering a sail. There are several types of sail controls that can change the shape of a sail and improve a boat's performance. With an infinite number of sail shape possibilities, optimizing your sails for the immediate conditions is the benchmark of a good sailor.

GENERAL RULES FOR SAIL CONTROLS

- When it comes to sail shape and power, deeper (fuller) sails have more power; flatter sails have less power.
- Sail controls are set looser in medium wind and tighter in very light and also in heavy wind.
- Generally, adjustments are made in small amounts or incrementally—not maximum on or all off.
- Watch the adjustment being made for the correct setting, not your hands pulling the controls.

ASSESSING SAIL SHAPE

The ability to make informed decisions about sail shape is one of the most important aspects of controlling a sailboat. Two key elements go into defining sail shape: draft and twist.

DRAFT: *Draft* describes the depth and location of the curvature in a sail. The draft is controlled by the outhaul, Cunningham/downhaul, backstay, sprit or main halyard. More tension on any of these controls reduces depth and moves the curvature forward. Easing these sail controls increases depth and moves the curvature aft.

TWIST: *Twist* describes the curvature of the leech, most noticeably near the top batten. Twist is most commonly controlled by the boom vang, traveler, mainsheet, Cunningham/downhaul or backstay. More tension on all of these controls, except the backstay, causes the leech to curl to windward and decreases twist; more tension on the backstay increases twist. The optimal setting on most boats is when the top batten is parallel with the boom. Wind pressure on the sail changes upwind and downwind, so the boom vang in particular will need adjustment if a boat changes course relative to the wind.

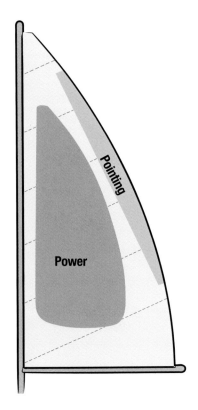

USING SAIL CONTROLS FOR UPWIND SAILING

Dinghies generally sail best and most efficiently when they are kept flat when heading upwind. When a boat's crew weight can no longer keep the boat flat when sailing upwind, the sails should be flattened to reduce power. At the moment the crew weight can keep the boat flat again, the sails are adjusted properly. If the wind strength changes, use the sail controls to reshape the sails for optimal performance.

SPEED MODE/POINT MODE: The flatter the sail shape and tighter the leech, the closer the boat will sail, or *point*, toward the wind. The trade-off is that flat sails are not as powerful. If the leech is so tight that the top batten curls to windward, the sail will stall and slow down. If the situation calls for pointing high (for example, pointing above an obstruction), make the sails flatter. If pointing high is less important than going fast through the water, make the sails fuller.

FLAT WATER VS. WAVES: When the boat is sailing upwind in waves, it needs more power. When the water is smooth, the boat requires less power to move through the water. If the boat doesn't need extra power in smooth water, it is good to flatten the sails and point high. As the waves build, it is important to put more power back into the boat by making the sails slightly fuller.

Adjustments to depower your sails include:
- Tightening the outhaul
- Bending the mast
- Moving the jib leads aft
- Putting Cunningham/downhaul on
- Tightening halyards

Reversing these controls will power up the sails.

MAINSHEET
The mainsheet performs two functions:
- Adjusting the mainsail in or out
- When sailing upwind, controlling the tightness of the leech

As the mainsail gets closer to the boat's centerline, the mainsheet pulls down on the boom, much like the boom vang. Sailors need to be conscious of mainsheet tension so they do not tighten the leech excessively and cause it to hook to windward. End-boom sheeting has a greater effect on leech tension than mid-boom sheeting because of the end-boom lever effect. Mainsheet tension also affects your forestay tension; pulling hard on the mainsheet pulls back on the mast and thus tightens the forestay.

TIP

▶ Leech tension directly affects the ability of a boat to point closer to the wind.

OUTHAUL: The outhaul pulls the sail *out* along the boom and controls the depth and location of the draft in a sail. More outhaul tension creates a flatter sail with a draft closer to the luff, which is better for pointing in very light or heavy wind conditions. Less outhaul tension creates a fuller sail with deep-draft power, which is better through waves or sailing in medium wind conditions.

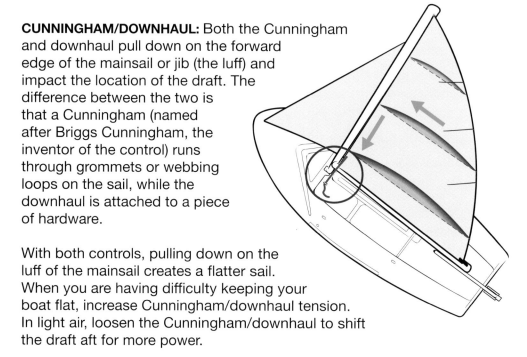

If the boat needs more power to sail through waves, or if the boat can be sailed flat, consider loosening the outhaul for more power. If the sailing conditions have small waves or no waves, or you are not able to keep the boat flat by hiking, tighten the outhaul. At a minimum, when you are sailing upwind, put enough tension on the outhaul to remove any vertical wrinkles along the foot of the sail.

CUNNINGHAM/DOWNHAUL: Both the Cunningham and downhaul pull down on the forward edge of the mainsail or jib (the luff) and impact the location of the draft. The difference between the two is that a Cunningham (named after Briggs Cunningham, the inventor of the control) runs through grommets or webbing loops on the sail, while the downhaul is attached to a piece of hardware.

With both controls, pulling down on the luff of the mainsail creates a flatter sail. When you are having difficulty keeping your boat flat, increase Cunningham/downhaul tension. In light air, loosen the Cunningham/downhaul to shift the draft aft for more power.

On some boats, halyard tension is used to adjust the draft location instead of a Cunningham or downhaul.

TIP

▶ Most sailors tighten the Cunningham to the point where the tension almost makes a vertical crease along the luff of the sail.

BOOM VANG: The boom vang, or vang, affects sail shape by altering leech tension and mast bend. The vang is the secondary means of controlling leech tension, after the mainsheet.

Tightening the boom vang puts more tension on the leech of the sail. When you tension the leech you close the leech, causing it to curl more to windward and reducing twist.

Upwind sailors tighten the boom vang so the battens are parallel with the boom. The way to sight this is to position yourself underneath the boom while you are sailing and look up at the windward side of the boom and the sail. If the outer edge of the battens point to windward, the boom vang is too tight and needs to be loosened; battens that are parallel to the boom allow the boat to point higher on a close hauled course.

When you are going upwind in heavy air conditions, pull the boom vang on hard. This will help flatten the sail by reducing draft and minimizing power to make the boat more stable and controllable. This is referred to as *vang sheeting*. Vang sheeting allows you to ease the mainsheet without losing leech tension; in effect, you are spilling excess pressure without losing the ability to point.

If the boat is being overpowered in very heavy air, consider increasing twist a lot by loosening the boom vang or tightening the backstay to depower the sail.

In light air, the boom vang may be left cleated without tension because the weight of the boom will likely eliminate all twist. Just a little twist in the leech allows the wind to flow smoothly along the sail and creates more power for upwind sailing.

TRAVELERS AND BRIDLES: Travelers and bridles are used to control the location of the boom relative to the centerline of the boat and the angle of the mainsheet to the wind. A traveler uses a car on a track that is adjusted using control lines to move it from side to side and change the position of the boom. A bridle (as on a 420) is a fixed piece of line that when shortened or lengthened affects the boom position relative to the boat's centerline.

Pulling the traveler to windward of centerline, or lengthening the bridle, enables the sailor to center the boom to achieve an efficient and powerful close hauled course. Easing the traveler car to leeward, or tightening the bridle, depowers the mainsail when you are sailing on a close hauled course and on close reaches.

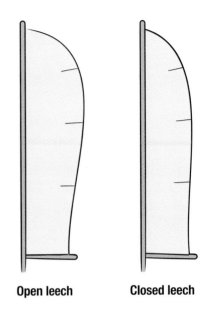

Open leech   Closed leech

TIP

▶ A looser boom vang that opens the leech slightly will provide speed but sacrifice pointing ability.

▶ A tight boom vang will be slower, but it could benefit pointing ability (until the sail stalls and wind doesn't flow over the sail).

BACKSTAY : The backstay is the standing rigging that runs from the top of the mast to the transom on some boats (typically larger daysailing dinghies and keelboats). It is typically made of wire, and on some boats it can be adjusted.

The backstay pulls the top of the mast aft. It is used to:
- Control the shape and leech of the main, thereby adding or reducing power
- Control the shape of the jib through headstay/jib luff sag
- Reduce the mainsail draft by bending the middle of the mast

Ease the backstay to increase sag in the jib luff, which makes the jib fuller and gives it more power. Tighten the backstay to reduce sag and make the jib flatter, which enables the boat to sail a little closer to the wind.

FULL LENGTH BATTENS: Some boats have battens that extend from the luff to the leech of the main. These are called *compression battens*. The depth of the sail can be altered depending on how tight the batten is pushed into its pocket. The more the batten is compressed, the more it will curve and force a deeper shape into the sail. Some boats will have a single full length batten in the top pocket (such as a 420 or a 470).

JIB HALYARD: Jib halyard controls jib luff tension. It is similar to the downhaul on the main sail and often described as luff sag (the looser the halyard, the more jib luff sag).
- When the halyard is pulled tight, the draft moves forward and the jib will have a flatter shape.
- When the halyard is eased, the draft moves aft and the jib will have a fuller and more powerful shape.

When determining correct jib tension, pull on the halyard until the rig is firm. Too little jib halyard and the rig will feel loose, sloppy and bounce around. Too much jib halyard tension and you may see the top of the mast bend toward the bow (called inverting). Jib luff tension can also be changed by a jib Cunningham/downhaul or a backstay, both of which have the same effect as the halyard. More tension results in a flatter jib.

JIB LEADS: Jib leads control available jib leech and foot tension. Not all boats with jibs have adjustable jib leads.
- When the lead is forward and jib sheet trimmed in, there will be more leech tension and a fuller foot-settings that power up the sail.
- When the lead is aft and jib sheet trimmed in, there will be more tension across the foot and a more open leech-settings that depower the sail.

USING SAIL CONTROLS FOR DOWNWIND SAILING

SAIL AND BOATHANDLING CONTROLS: When sailing downwind, as sails shift from pull mode to push mode, there is a need for deeper, more powerful sails. The Cunningham/downhaul should be eased and the boom vang and outhaul loosened. The draft will then be at its deepest spot, in the middle of the sail.

Since the boom vang controls the tension of the leech, when the boat turns downwind it is necessary to adjust the vang appropriately for the wind velocity. Ease the boom vang so the top batten is parallel with the boom. If the vang is too tight when the boat starts sailing downwind, the leech will likely hook to windward (hinging on the inboard end of the battens); if the vang is too loose, the leech will twist open too much or even cause the boat to become unstable. The sail may also chafe and tear on the rigging.

The outhaul controls the draft of the sail. When sailing downwind, a fuller draft with its deepest point in the middle of the sail is best for increased power. On a reach, the outhaul can be eased slightly compared to upwind sailing. As the boat heads down to a broad reach or run, the draft can move farther back still, until the deepest part of the sail is nearly 50% of the way back from the luff. Remember to retension the outhaul if you head up and sail upwind; if it is left loose, the boat's performance will suffer.

TIP

▶ Don't forget that you can pull the underwater foils (centerboard/daggerboard) up about half-way when sailing downwind; this reduces friction in the water. Leave enough of the board down to steer comfortably and keep the boat tracking straight ahead.

CHAPTER 4

HOW SAILING WORKS

▶ The Science of Sailing
▶ How a Sail Works
▶ How a Foil Works
▶ Balance: How Sails and Foils Work Together
▶ Weather Helm
▶ Lee Helm

THE SCIENCE OF SAILING

For a beginning sailor, getting a boat to move is solved by trimming the sails, steering with the rudder and avoiding the No-Go Zone. Once you have mastered the beginning learn-to-sail skills, understanding the basic science that makes a sailboat work will allow you to become a better sailor and make decisions about rigging and sail adjustments, sail trim, weight placement and steering.

HOW A SAIL WORKS

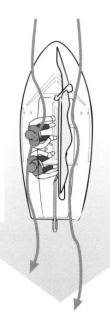

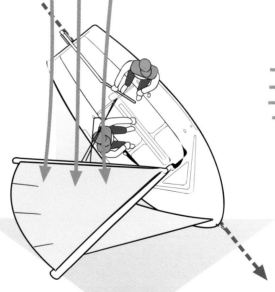

NO-GO
A sailboat cannot sail directly into the wind. You can try it, but your sails will only flap (luff) and you'll be dead in the water...or even start moving backward. Because there is no difference in wind pressure between one side of the sail and the other, the sail cannot generate either "push" or "pull." No push... no pull...NO GO!

PUSH MODE
With the wind coming from behind, the sail (and boat) are simply pushed forward through the water.

If you hold your hand out the window of a moving car with your palm facing the wind, you can feel the wind "push" your hand back. This is how a sail works when the wind is coming from behind.

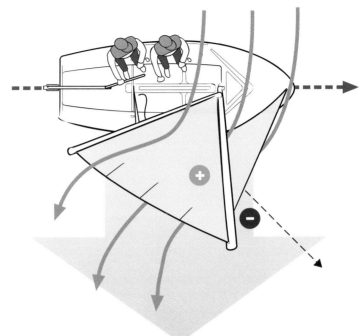

If you hold your hand out the window of a moving car, you can feel the force of the wind lifting your hand. This is the same force that "pulls" a sailboat forward when the wind comes over the side of the boat.

PULL MODE

Your sail is much more efficient at using the wind than your hand. It is shaped to bend the wind as it flows by, creating higher pressure on the inside of the sail ⊕ and lower pressure on the outside ⊖, thus creating lift. The lift the sail creates "pulls" the boat forward and sideways. The boat's *keel* keeps the boat from being pulled sideways through the water.

HOW A FOIL WORKS

If sails are a boat's engine, then the centerboard and rudder are the boat's tires: they provide the grip necessary to keep you on track. The centerboard and rudder create *lift* in much the same way that a sail does. When a sailboat is sailing upwind, it continually slips slightly to leeward.

When sailing downwind, sideways force from the sails is lessened so you do not need as much centerboard. Raising the centerboard for downwind sailing reduces the amount of drag, which increases boat speed.

While a centerboard's primary responsibility is resistance to side-slipping, a rudder's primary function is steering. By moving the rudder to one side of the boat or the other, pressure on the rudder blade provides the force to steer the boat. Remember that every time the rudder is moved from a neutral position amidships, the force to steer will also slow the boat down. Less helm usage usually allows the boat to sail faster.

CHAPTER 4

BOAT BALANCE

Center of Lateral Resistance
Center of Lateral Resistance is the focal point of all the forces resisting slipping sideways through the water.

Center of Effort is the theoretical focal point of the force generated by the wind acting on the sail(s).

Drag is a slowing force resulting from the friction of a boat moving through the water.

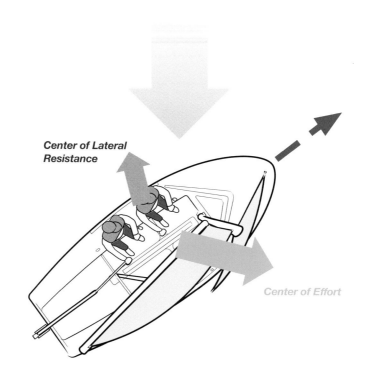

Center of Lateral Resistance

Center of Effort

HOW SAILS AND FOILS WORK TOGETHER

When the lift generated by the sails is combined with the lift of the underwater foils, the resultant force moves the boat straight ahead. (In actuality, a sailboat always goes just a tad sideways.) When the underwater foils are not optimized and made fair and smooth, the flow of water is disturbed and the foils develop drag through the water. This drag reduces the amount of lift and the boat slips more to leeward.

You can steer a boat with its sails, crew weight or rudder—or a combination of these—because of a principle called **balance**. A sailboat is a collection of forces in motion, not all of which are headed in the same direction. There are forces exerted by the mainsail and the jib, both of which pull the boat forward and sideways; the location of this collective force is referred to as **Center of Effort**. There are opposing forces exerted by the water on the keel and rudder, and the location of this collective force is referred to as **Center of Lateral Resistance**.

When all of these forces are *in balance*, the boat will sail forward in a straight line. If they are not, the boat will want to turn.

This is why you are able to steer the boat by trimming in or easing your sails or, as you will learn in the next chapter, by moving your crew weight. By doing so, you are consciously throwing the boat *out of balance*.

As your sailing skills improve, you will use the principle of balance more and more to get the best performance out of your boat and execute more advanced maneuvers. For now, just understanding balance will help explain why certain things are happening on your boat.

WEATHER HELM

As sailors, we have all experienced *weather helm*—whether we knew that term or not. Weather helm occurs when sailing upwind in strong or puffy wind. The boat turns to windward, even though the rudder may even be bending hard to windward to try to counteract the boat's turning. Sailors experience weather helm because the force in the mainsail overpowers the jib (if the boat is sloop-rigged) and rudder by moving the Center of Effort backward in the boat and to leeward of the Center of Lateral Resistance, which causes the boat to lose balance.

Weather helm is easily recognized by the tiller being pulled hard to windward, often bending under the pressure, while trying to sail a straight line upwind. Weather helm slows a boat down considerably, largely because of the overuse of the rudder. The proper correction is to ease the mainsheet, hike harder to windward, flatten the mainsail's shape with sail controls, or pull up the centerboard or daggerboard as needed (up to 25%).

LEE HELM

Lee helm is the opposite of weather helm. A boat's tendency to turn to leeward is caused by too little force in the mainsail combined with too much weight on the windward side, thus the Center of Effort has moved forward in the boat and to windward of the Center of Lateral Resistance. Most frequently this occurs when sailing in light wind conditions, or when sailing out of a puff or into the lee of an obstruction. The proper correction is first to flatten the boat by moving the crew's weight leeward, move the tiller to leeward, adjust the mainsail so it is fuller and deeper and make sure the centerboard or daggerboard is all the way down.

CHAPTER 5

BODY POSITION

▶ Side-to-Side Position for Upwind
▶ Side-to-Side Position for Downwind
▶ Fore and Aft Position for Upwind
▶ Fore and Aft Position for Downwind
▶ Hiking Techniques
▶ Holding the Tiller Extension and Mainsheet
▶ Handling Lines

TIP

▶ To learn proper fore and aft trim, try sitting as far forward and aft as possible so you can see the extremes. Remember to adjust your position as conditions change!

For a beginning sailor, just having the boat upright can be a success. As a sailor improves there is more to consider about body position to sail a boat well. Where you choose to sit and move while sailing will impact how fast a boat will move and how comfortable everyone will be onboard. Learning how to use your weight and position in the boat enables you to sail the boat properly and quickly. Depending on wind strength, environmental conditions and the boat you are sailing, your body position will help keep your boat sailing in optimum balance.

SIDE-TO-SIDE POSITION FOR UPWIND

Most sailboats, with the exception of boats that have a hard chine, sail upwind best when they are nearly or completely flat and not heeling. A nearly vertical centerboard or daggerboard does its best job in preventing a sailboat from slipping sideways, allowing you the most significant progress toward your windward destination.

To keep the boat flat, the skipper and crew adjust their weight from one side of the boat to the other, depending on how strong the wind is blowing.

The crew moves the most to keep the boat flat, allowing the skipper to sit still and focus on steering. Whenever you need to move, lean with your upper body first, then step lightly and quickly to move your whole body as needed (or in anticipation of the boat heeling more).

The skipper will find that a sailboat may steer a little better with a little heel in light air. Heeling to leeward in light air will also keep your sail shape optimal rather than luffing back and forth. So when you are sailing in light air, only heel the boat enough to give the skipper a good feel for the helm and to keep the sails in the right shape.

Catamarans sail best upwind when they have the windward pontoon "flying" just above the water. This reduces wetted surface friction and allows the boat to sail faster.

SIDE-TO-SIDE POSITION FOR DOWNWIND

When we sail downwind, the force of the wind on the sails is pushing in the same direction the boat is sailing in. There is less of a need to keep the boat flat and less of a need to keep the centerboard or daggerboard vertical in the water to prevent side-slipping.

Instead, the centerboard or daggerboard functions as the pivot point for steering. Without a need for a vertical centerboard or daggerboard, you can retract the centerboard or daggerboard part way and heel the boat to windward; this reduces the friction of wetted surface and gets the sail up higher into the wind. This is referred to as *windward heel*. The skipper should sit on the windward rail and the crew should adjust his or her weight to maintain a consistent windward heel.

FORE AND AFT POSITIONS FOR UPWIND

The skipper and crew will improve the performance of the boat if they adjust the place they are sitting in the boat for the existing wind and wave conditions. If you move too far forward, the bow of the boat will dig into each wave like a snowplow. If you sit too far aft, the stern will sink lower and displace more water. In either situation, the boat will slow down as a result of improper fore and aft position.

While there will be differences in every type of boat, the starting place in medium air and flat seas is for the skipper to sit just aft of the spot where the mainsheet is trimmed. If there is a crewmember aboard, he or she should sit shoulder to shoulder in front of the skipper.

The knuckle, or curve on the bow of the hull, should be in the water just a little bit. For flat bows, such as prams, the flat section where the bow meets the bottom of the hull should be just above the water surface.

In light winds and flat water, moving forward to get more of the stern out of the water will improve the boat's speed. Do not move so far forward that the bow is digging too deeply and moving a lot of water.

In heavier winds and larger waves, the crew will need to move farther aft from the original starting place for medium wind. This helps keep the bow out of oncoming waves and helps keep the sails and underwater foils in balance, making the boat easier to sail. As the wind increases, or the hull speed increases, the skipper and crew will need to move farther aft to keep the bow up.

FORE AND AFT POSITIONS FOR DOWNWIND

When a boat sails downwind on a reach or run, the weight of the crew may need to move aft, especially in higher wind and planing conditions. If the boat is able to plane, the skipper and crew should slide farther aft to get the bow out of the water. Remember to move forward again when you turn to sail upwind.

HIKING TECHNIQUES

As wind velocity increases or decreases, sailors must adjust their weight to keep the boat flat. Hiking is one method used to keep the boat balanced and nearly flat. In a doublehanded boat, the crew is the first to make adjustments; if the crew can make all the necessary movement required to keep the boat flat, the skipper can stay put and focus on steering. As a change in wind velocity approaches, start adjusting weight placement before the change actually occurs and be ready to move more as needed. Keeping the boat flat decreases sideways slippage and allows you to reach your destination more efficiently.

Photo: Justin Chando

As a general rule, most sailors like to hike out with the middle of the back of their thigh (between the knee and hip) on the edge of the side of the boat. The top of your feet, just behind your toes, should be positioned under the hiking strap and close together. Hiking straps are adjustable and can be tightened or loosened for comfort. It is important that you are comfortable, because you may end up in this position for a while. Closed-toe shoes or boots should be worn to protect your feet while you are hiking; sandals and loose fitting shoes will be more of a hindrance, especially if you capsize and they come off your feet.

Through continued practice sailors learn how to hike straight-legged for long periods of time. Straight-legged hiking extends your body out the farthest, counteracting the pressure on the sails to create the best boat speed. When sailors stop hiking straight-legged and sit on the rail of the boat instead, the boat will heel more and slow down.

CHAPTER 5

Photo: Justin Chando

While a straight upper body in addition to straight legs is fastest, most sailors adopt a more comfortable position that allows them to see better and hike longer. They keep their upper body more upright, just about perpendicular to the surface of the water. Both the skipper and crew will want to look forward while hiking or sitting on the side of the boat to see the sails, upcoming changes in the wind, and other boats or hazards.

HOLDING THE TILLER EXTENSION AND MAINSHEET

A skipper should assume a hand and body position to steer and trim sails most effectively. By placing your hands in front of you, with thumb side up, grasp the tiller extension as if you are holding a microphone and keep your elbows at your sides as you grip the mainsheet. In this position, you will be using the strongest muscles in your arms—your forearms and biceps—to control the tiller and sheets. Plus, your compact body stance will be in the most comfortable and relaxed position to enable you to focus on sailing the boat.

HANDLING LINES

Be sure that you never wrap a line around your hands or hold it with your teeth. When holding a line under pressure you should be able to release the line just by relaxing your grip and letting the line fall. It is important to be able to release a line quickly so you can easily swim free of the boat in the event of a capsize.

CLOSE HAULED AND UPWIND SAILING

▶ Refining Upwind Sailing
▶ Roll Tacking

REFINING UPWIND SAILING

Close hauled sailing is the position defined as closest to the wind. Inside of being close hauled, there are some subtly different positions that allow you to increase and improve your upwind performance—depending on the wind and wave conditions.

A boat can be sailed high when you are sailing close hauled, to a point closer to the wind and perhaps even entering into the edge of the No-Go Zone. Pointing high, however, depletes the sails of good wind flow and slows the boat down. A boat can also be sailed on the low side of a close hauled course, almost down to a close reach position. When sailing low, a boat has increased wind power in the sails and will sail faster, but you sacrifice pointing toward the wind as a result. Usually, sailing a high or low close hauled course is done temporarily to sail above a mark (high) or in anticipation of the wake from a powerboat (low).

THE GROOVE: As you steer upwind, you will react to changes in wind speed and direction by steering the boat either toward or away from the wind, while keeping the telltales flowing back smoothly. *The groove* is the course between the high and low side of close hauled, when you are making the best speed and achieving the highest pointing angle toward the wind.

When you are in the groove the helm is neutral, the telltales on the jib are streaming on both sides and the boat is sailing at the correct angle of heel. Far from a compromise, when sailing in the groove the boat just feels right.

PUFFS AND LULLS: A beginning sailor reacts to changes in the wind's velocity or direction. An intermediate sailor should try to anticipate changes in the wind and then make adjustments in weight placement and sail trim for better boat performance. Keep an eye upwind and on the surface of the water to anticipate changes. Look for wind indicators upwind that provide clues about the wind's strength and direction. The way sails are trimmed through puffs and lulls will directly impact the way a skipper steers. The impact of a puff, which causes a boat to heel and round up, can be minimized by easing the sails (usually just the mainsail). Conversely, trimming the mainsail back in while exiting a puff will keep the boat properly powered.

CHAPTER 6

Unless there is an overpowering puff or you are close reaching, the jib is left alone. The skipper is steering their close hauled course based on the trim of the jib; if the jib is eased, the skipper may end up steering onto a close reach instead of staying on a close hauled course.

As you become more comfortable with identifying puffs, you will begin to use the *Ease–Hike–Trim* method. As you feel the puff begin to affect your boat, *Ease* the sail slightly as you feather the boat, *Hike* the boat flat for the duration of the puff, and *Trim* the sails back in to power up once you are in full control.

FEATHERING: When a boat is initially hit by a puff, the boat will typically heel and round up toward the No-Go Zone; the net result is most frequently a slowing of the boat. When a sailor anticipates a puff, he or she assesses the impact of a puff and with a small tiller adjustment intentionally steers the boat toward the No-Go Zone, to the point where the sails luff slightly. This eases the impact of the puff. As the boat sails out of the puff, the skipper heads down to the groove. Repeating this cycle, scalloping slightly toward the No-Go Zone for each puff and returning to the groove as the puff abates, is known as *feathering*.

FOOTING: Footing powers up the boat when you are sailing a close hauled course. In situations such as going over a big wave or sailing in light wind conditions, more power is needed. Easing sails slightly and heading down to the lower side of the groove, perhaps even into a close reach, provides more power.

TIP

Follow these general rules for handling puffs and lulls :

▶ **Puffs:** Prepare for a puff by easing the mainsail and feathering, simultaneously combined with an anticipatory hike.

▶ **Lulls:** Prepare for a lull with an anticipatory move inboard and to leeward, simultaneously easing the sails while footing.

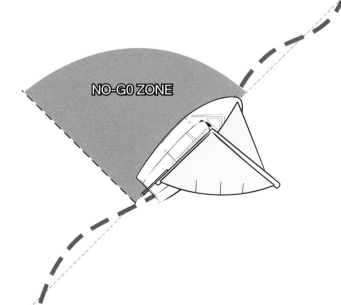

STEERING: It is necessary to steer with the tiller to go in the desired direction. However, overusing the tiller results in slowing your boat down. Every time the tiller is moved to one side of the boat or the other, it causes drag or turbulence. Drag is increased friction of the boat moving through the water. This is created by unequal pressure from water flowing past the rudder. A neutral helm, usually when the tiller is in the middle of the boat, is when there is the least amount of drag on the rudder. Minimizing tiller movement to essential steering needs helps to keep a boat moving quickly.

Developing a feel for how much helm is needed takes practice. Actively heading up a little in a puff (feathering), eases the effect of the increased wind velocity; heading down in a lull (footing) increases pressure in the sails to keep the boat moving fast. Once the puff or lull passes, the skipper steers the boat into the groove again to keep the boat moving efficiently through puffs and lulls. Correct use of body placement and sail trim can minimize the amount of tiller movement required to keep the boat sailing close hauled efficiently and quickly.

Roll Tacking

The transition from one tack to another is inherently slow as the sails luff through the No-Go Zone and the boat turns a roughly 90° arc. Quickening the pace at which a boat turns through the No-Go Zone will reduce the time needed to pass through the 90° arc and improve acceleration once the boat has tacked. Most of the steps to roll tack are identical to a regular tack, with the following additions:

1. The sailors prepare to tack as normal, making sure they have speed and are sailing a close hauled course.
2. The boat is tacked while the sailors remain on the same side of the boat. The crew backwinds the jib until the bow had crossed through head-to-wind. When the jib is able to fill on the new tack, the crew trims in the new jib sheet without letting the jib luff.

3a. In one smooth motion, the skipper makes the first move to quickly cross the boat by leading with the aft-most foot first, performing a behind-the-back hand pass of the tiller and mainsheet, and then sitting down on the rail and getting their feet under the hiking straps.
3b. Just after the skipper starts to cross the boat and the rail has touched the water, the crew launches across the boat to the opposite side to assist the skipper in flattening the boat. The skipper and crew should both sit on the other side of the boat at the same time.

4. Skipper and crew hike to promptly flatten the boat until the mast is vertical again. In light wind conditions, the crew might only need to lean over the rail, and prepare to sit on the seat as the skipper flattens the boat from the rail.

CHAPTER 7

JIBING TECHNIQUES AND DOWNWIND SAILING

▶ Speed Is Your Friend
▶ Methods for Quicker Sail Transition
▶ Steering Jibes
▶ Roll Jibing
▶ Avoiding Capsizes to Windward

While a boat sails through a jibe faster than it does during a tack, there are boathandling skills that will increase the efficiency and safety of a jibe. This section addresses the key components for keeping your boat upright and travelling fast during jibes.

SPEED IS YOUR FRIEND

Sailors often feel as if they have more control of a boat when it is moving slowly. In many situations, such as docking or approaching a person in the water, slower speeds are preferable. However, when sailing downwind and jibing, it is safer to have the boat moving as fast as possible. Remember that a jibe occurs when your boat is sailing downwind and in the same direction as the wind.

The faster you can keep the boat moving while jibing, the closer the boat's speed will be to the wind speed. If the boat keeps up with the wind speed, the boom will swing across more slowly. If the boat slows down, the wind will force the boom to go across faster and with more power.

When you can perfect this technique, you will look forward to jibing in heavy wind.

METHODS FOR QUICKER SAIL TRANSITION

Both the mainsail and jib can be handled to keep a boat's speed up while jibing. The goal is to reduce the amount of time the sails are luffing or not working at maximum efficiency.

JIB: When performing a jibe, the crew's goals are to use their weight to keep the boat flat, to switch the jib from one side of the boat to the other, and to keep the jib full as much as possible. For a jibe, keep the jib full as long as you can while grabbing the new sheet and removing any slack. Once the boat has settled after the jibe, find the optimum body position to keep the boat flat and trim the jib properly to the new course.

TIP

Before a boat is jibed, some adjustments need to be made so the boat will perform and steer better.

▶ The centerboard/ daggerboard should be lowered and the boom vang should be tensioned to keep the boom from rising.

▶ Once the jibe is complete, the centerboard/ daggerboard and boom vang can be adjusted back to their respective downwind settings.

MAINSAIL: Before the jibe, the boat will be sailing on a deep reach or run. The mainsail should be no less than three-quarters of the way out to the shroud. To keep the boat moving quickly, the mainsail needs to stay far out and catch wind. Trimming the sail in to the middle of the boat is safe in light to moderate breeze, but it is not as efficient or effective as leaving the sail out to catch the wind. The skipper will alert their crew to a jibe, confirm that everyone is ready, initiate the turn, then grab the multiple parts of the mainsheet to pull the mainsail across the boat with a snap or jerk while *ducking* under the boom as the sail comes across.

STEERING JIBES

C-TURN: It may be helpful to think of steering the boat in an elongated letter "C" in most jibing situations. The pace at which the boat turns should be consistent until the sails and sailors cross sides. The tiller only needs to be turned a little to make the jibe smooth and controlled. The turn should be significantly smaller and less dramatic than when tacking; the boat is only turning through 15° to 25° in a jibe, compared to 90° in a tack.

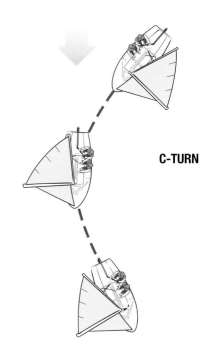

C-TURN

S-TURN: S-turns, or safety jibes, are useful for jibing in heavier winds. As described earlier, when the wind speed increases the sudden impact when the mainsail transitions from one side to the other also increases. In light and moderate wind speeds, sailors maintain control of the boat by keeping it heading straight after the mainsail transitions by using their weight and the rudder. As the wind speed increases, the sudden impact on the sail pushes the boat to round up suddenly. Rounding up is like heading up, but it is out of control and carries a high risk of causing a capsize if the boom hits the water. There is a way for a skipper to counteract rounding up by using an S-turn.

A key point to remember is that jibing is an *action* rather than a *reaction* to the boat and sail movements. To perform an S-turn, the skipper will follow all the steps previously outlined for a jibe until the sail crosses the boat. At the instant the sail crosses, the skipper reverses the tiller slightly and steers slightly back into the jibe. However, remember that if you turn too far, the boat will jibe back; if you turn too little, the boat will round up. Each boat requires a different amount of counter-turn, depending on wind strength and boat type.

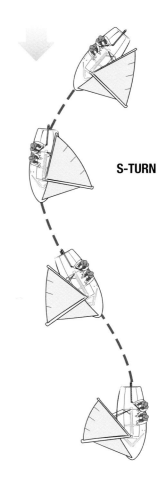

S-TURN

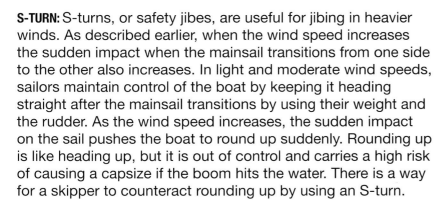

CHAPTER 7

ROLL JIBING

Roll jibing, like roll tacking, improves the efficiency of a transitional maneuver. Roll jibing makes the boat jibe faster, allowing for less time with the mainsail in transition from one tack to the other, while minimizing use of the rudder. Roll jibes are most useful in light and medium air; the maneuver becomes less effective, dangerous and unnecessary as the breeze builds.

① Preparation
- Helmsman makes sure it is clear to jibe.
- Helmsman and crew communicate as crew prepares windward jib sheet.

② Initiation
- Helmsman turns rudder slowly and smoothly.
- Helmsman and crew hike to windward so the rail they are sitting on touches the water surface.

③ Transition – Mainsail crosses the boat
- Using the mainsheet (or its parts) the skipper snaps the mainsheet across the boat then switches sides.
- Crew releases jib, and quickly begins to move across while trimming the new jib sheet.

④ Recovery
- Crew hikes hard to bring the boat back to flat.
- Helmsman sits and trims the main and centers the rudder slowly and smoothly.

⑤ Completion
- Helmsman and crew work to trim the main and jib correctly.
- Helmsman and crew communicate.

WIND

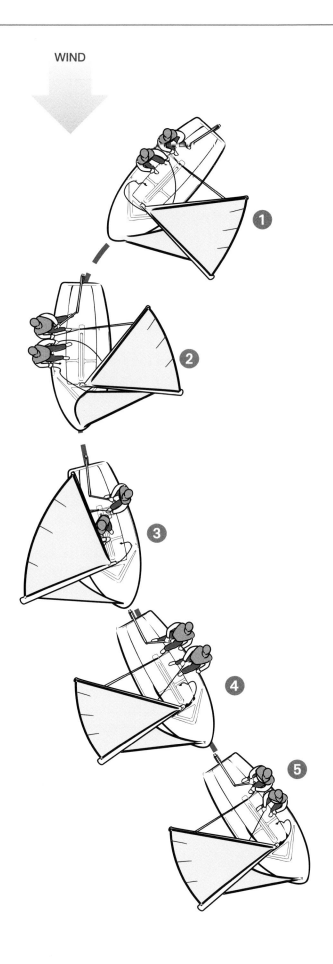

The most important thing to remember in roll jibing is to duck when the boom comes across. The timing of a roll jibe results in sailors and the boom crossing the boat nearly simultaneously, so remember to stay low while crossing the boat.

The preparation leading into the jibe is unchanged from beginning sailing. The skipper warns of the upcoming maneuver. The crew responds when ready. The boat is turned into the jibe. It is at this point that things deviate slightly. Instead of crossing the boat in advance or after the sail switches sides, the sailors will stay seated until the rail touches the water's surface, causing the boat to heel to windward. The amount of heel is determined by the ability of the crew to spring up to the new windward side of the boat to level it out again. Usually, it is the crew's responsibility to hike harder during the roll, allowing the skipper to cross slightly ahead of the crew. This is preferable because it allows the skipper to steer more effectively.

To perform a roll jibe well, sailors will add the methods for quicker sail transitions mentioned above and keep the boat moving quickly. Coordinating the efforts of each sailor into one team takes practice. Good communication, good boathandling and practice will improve your ability to roll jibe.

WIND

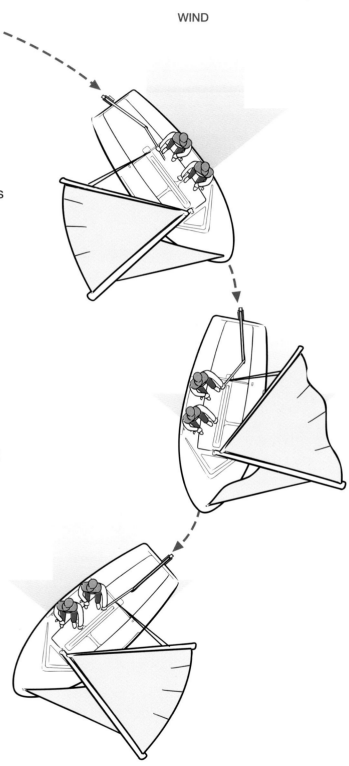

CHAPTER 7

AVOIDING CAPSIZES TO WINDWARD

A windward capsize occurs when sailing on a run, usually in moderate to heavy wind. Typically, a windward capsize is caused by the boat becoming unstable and rolling back and forth. If the boat heels to windward too much and the sailors do not respond quickly enough or overreact, the boat can capsize to windward with significantly more force than a capsize to leeward.

To avoid a capsize to windward, keep your boom vang tight enough to reduce twist at the top of the mainsail (which will help depower the sail) and keep your centerboard lower than you would in lighter air. If the boat begins to roll, head up slightly until the sails start to luff or slightly trim your mainsheet. Any of these techniques will help keep your boat more stable, but combining them is the best solution.

WIND

WIND

Factors that can cause a windward capsize while sailing downwind include:
- Mainsheet is too far out
- Boom vang is too loose
- Centerboard is too far up
- Sailor's weight is improperly placed
- Over-steering
- Increase in wind strength
- Inconsistent wave action

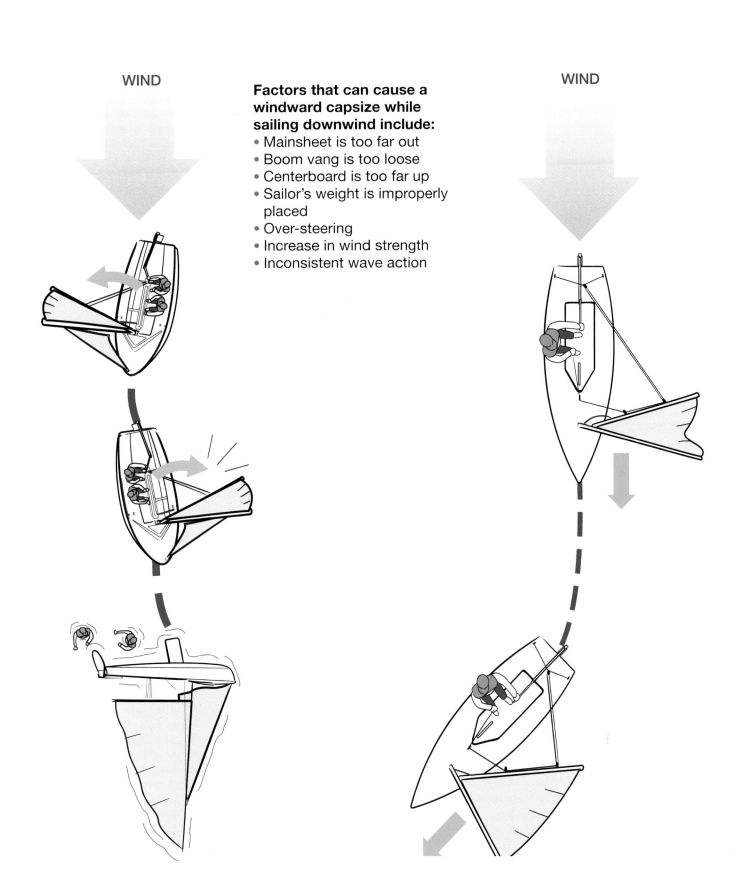

RIGGING AND SEAMANSHIP

▶ Knots
▶ Paddling and Sculling
▶ Shortening Sail
▶ Docking
▶ Anchoring
▶ Towing

There are several important skills that serve as a backup to sailing's endless variables. Knot tying, paddling, sculling, anchoring, towing, shortening sail and securing your boat alongside or onto a dock are maneuvers that every sailor will probably need to perform, sooner or later.

KNOTS

Just as every line has a specific purpose, every time you need a knot you'll want to use the right one. A good knot is secure with good holding power and can easily be untied. As a sailor who has already mastered the beginning learn-to-sail skills,

you already know several knots, including the bowline, figure eight and square knot. The following knots are important to know as an intermediate sailor.

There are a variety of knots appropriate to use as halyard knots. Sailors use bowlines, stopper-knots and even half hitches. Ideally your choice of knot will resist slipping, allow the sail to be hoisted to its maximum, and allow the halyard to lead directly from the knot at the center of the head of the sail.

Clove Hitch
A clove hitch is used to tie a line to an object. It is not a very secure knot. It is very easily untied and, with an extra half hitch, can be used to secure a tiller.

Round Turn and Two Half hitches
This knot uses a loop to secure a line to an object.

Clove Hitch

1 Wrap a loop of the end around the object.

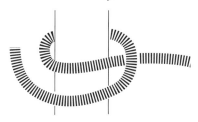

2 Cross over the standing part and wrap a second loop around the object.

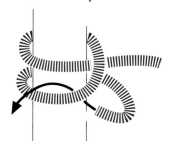

3 Tuck the end under the crossing you just made and tighten.

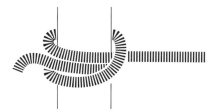

Round Turn and Two Half hitches

1 Wrap the end of the line twice around the object.

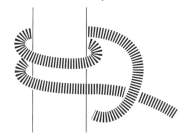

2 Cross the end over the outside of the standing part.

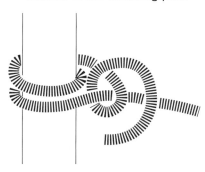

3 Use the end to tie two half hitches onto the standing part.

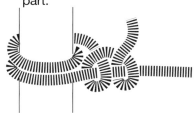

PADDLING AND SCULLING

When maneuvering near a dock or in other restricted areas, muscle power may be your safest and best method of propulsion. There are two ways a sailboat can be powered without using the sails: paddling or sculling. Paddling can be done for extended periods, while sculling is more often used for short distances.

Paddling works best with at least two people in the boat. One person steers with the rudder while the other paddles from the side of the boat. If the centerboard is all the way down, the boat will track nicely through the water and the paddler will only need to paddle from one side.

CHAPTER 8

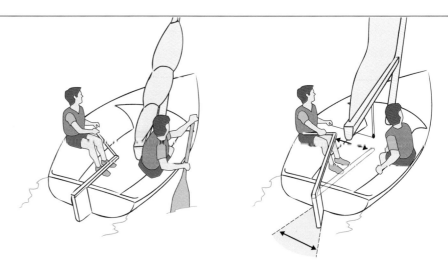

TIP

If the jib wire takes up the strain of the forestay to support the mast on your boat, DO NOT shorten sail by lowering the jib or the entire rig may collapse.

Club 420: The easiest way to shorten sail on a Club 420 is to cat-rig your boat. Attach the jib halyard to the jib tack pin and tighten the jib halyard.

Laser: The easiest way to shorten sail on a Laser is to disconnect the clew and Cunningham from the sail and wrap the sail around the mast several times. You should experiment with some of the techniques described to find what works best in different conditions.

Optimist: The easiest way to shorten sail on an Optimist is to remove the sprit pole, either tie the peak of the sail down using the sprit control line, or let the peak flap in the breeze. Make sure you secure the sprit in the boat.

For short distances, it is often easiest to scull the boat. In sculling, you move the tiller and rudder repeatedly back and forth, using it like a fish tail at the stern. If you have lowered the sails, they should be furled or stowed so they won't blow in the water or get in the way.

SHORTENING SAIL

When the wind is too strong and your boat is heeling too much, you should shorten your sail. Your boat will go just as fast and will be more in control with less sail area exposed to the wind. Different boats may require different techniques to reduce sail area.

LOWERING THE JIB: As long as the mast isn't supported by the jib wire, the easiest way to reduce sail is to simply lower the jib. With just the mainsail up, however, the boat is no longer in balance. The wind pressure on the mainsail will tend to rotate the bow of the boat toward the wind, and you will feel weather helm. To compensate, you will need to steer with the tiller pulled slightly away from the mainsail to keep the boat sailing straight. Not all boats will sail to windward with the jib down.

REEFING: The area of the mainsail may be reduced by lowering the sail partially and securing the lower portion to the boom. This is best accomplished while on a close reach or while hove-to with the mainsail luffing. (To learn how to heave-to, see the next chapter.)

LOWERING THE MAINSAIL: The most significant way you can reduce sail is to lower the mainsail. With just the jib up, however, the boat is longer in balance. The wind pressure on the jib will tend to rotate the bow away from the wind, and you will feel lee helm. To compensate, you will need to steer with the tiller slightly pushed towards the mainsail to keep the boat sailing straight.

DOCKING

Putting your boat away correctly will protect it and make it easier to use the next time you want to go sailing. Small centerboard dinghies are stored on top of floating docks in cradles. There are a couple of important steps you need to take to ensure that your boat is secure and properly put to bed.

- When pulling up on the dock, make sure the centerboard is pulled up or the daggerboard is up and put away. Remove any stern and tank plugs to allow collected water to drain and to prevent the boat from filling with water if it rains. Do not leave through-hull (Elvstrom-type) bailers in the open position as they are likely to be damaged.
- After removing your sails, make sure the halyards and sheets are cleated to prevent swinging booms and lost lines. Be certain that your control lines are properly coiled and secured. Leaving them in the bottom of the boat shortens their lifespan.
- Most places that leave the boats in cradles have a system for securing the boat to the dock. Typically, lines secure up and around the base of each shroud or through jib sheet fairleads. Follow the procedure carefully so that wind or waves won't knock the boat off its cradle. Some set-ups include tying the bow line down to a padeye or cleat on the dock.

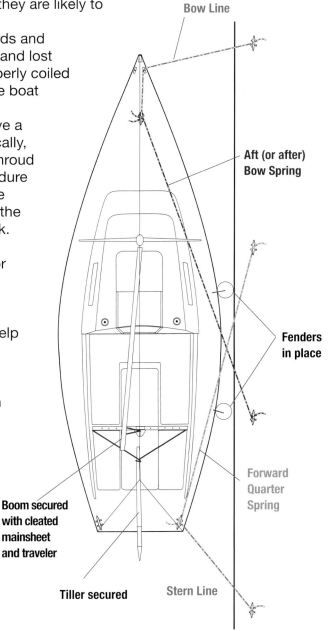

Bow Line

Aft (or after) Bow Spring

Fenders in place

Forward Quarter Spring

Boom secured with cleated mainsheet and traveler

Tiller secured

Stern Line

Dinghies are generally not tied up alongside docks for extended periods of time. Still, it is worth doing this correctly, to serve both as practice for when you are sailing other types of boats and for the safety and longevity of your boat. The following guidelines will help you when you need to tie up alongside a dock.

Secure your boat with a series of bow, stern and spring lines. Lead them from the boat to cleats on the dock.

- Bow and stern lines keep the boat close to the dock.
- Spring lines cross each other and keep the boat from moving forward and backward along the dock.
- Tie the boat so it is parallel to the dock.
- All cleated dock lines should be secured with a cleat hitch.
- Use fenders to protect the boat.
- Fenders should be placed amidships to prevent damage caused by the boat banging or chafing unnecessarily against the dock.
- Your fenders should be long enough to protect the boat's side, even in rough weather when there might be a fair bit of vertical movement due to waves.

ANCHORING

As in docking, preparation is the key to successful anchoring. Before anchoring, take down and stow the jib. Make sure the foredeck is clear except for the anchor and its line (***rode***), which should be coiled on the deck (laid out in large loops) so it will run freely. If there is a pulpit, make sure the anchor and rode will run under it.

WIND

The Danforth anchor is very common. It is strong, lightweight, holds well, and is easy to store.

❶ When everything is prepared, sail **on a reach**, about 3-6 boat lengths downwind of where you want to drop your anchor. When you are directly downwind of where you want to drop it, head up into the wind.

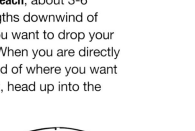

❷ **As the boat comes to a stop**, lower (do not throw or drop) the anchor. After it hits the bottom, pay out the anchor line as you drift back.

TIP

In ideal conditions you minimally want:
▶ 3 feet of rode for every foot of depth for a swim
▶ 5 feet of rode for every foot of depth for a picnic
▶ 7 feet of rode for every foot of depth if the boat will be left unattended or you are staying for an extended period

❸ **When you've reached the spot** where you want the boat to remain, firmly cleat off the rode. Check for adequate scope and that your anchor is holding. Then lower your mainsail.

TOWING

We all want to sail our boats using our own skill, but there are times when we need to be towed. Being towed is a skill just like any other in sailing—and no less important.

In order to be safely towed you will want to have a line at least three times as long as your boat. Tow lines (also referred to as *bow lines*) are typically made of Dacron (polyester). Floating line, such as polypropylene, can work for dinghies, but this type of line is not as strong as Dacron and breaks down over time in sunlight. When the line is under load during a tow, polypropylene may not be the best choice. Check your tow line regularly. It should be free of chafe, discoloration and knots.

Attach the tow line to a strong point on your boat. While some boats will have a cleat on or near the bow, or hardware on the bow chainplate to which the tow line can be secured, it is often not designed to take the load of a tow. Seek alternate attachment points for a towline, especially if there are multiple boats being towed. Dinghies that do not have a deck-stepped mast require the tow line to be secured around the mast with a bowline, after passing the tow line through a shackle or loop of line on the bow of the boat. Boats that have a deck-stepped mast should secure the towline around a stong structural part of the hull like the traveler bar.

The boom and sail should be stowed so the tiller is free to move from side to side. While under tow, follow the transom of the tow boat— or in the case of a tow set-up with multiple sailboats, the sailboat in front of you. It is important to pay attention to what is happening both inside and outside your boat at all times while you are under tow.

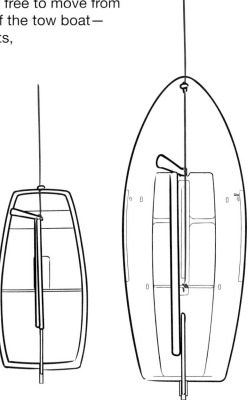

When coming off a tow, prepare to retrieve your line when it is cast off by the tow boat or the sailboat in front of you. Depending on your destination, you may need to remember that boats involved in a tow have limited maneuverability, so it is your responsibility to stay clear.

CAUTION: When preparing your boat for a tow, be sure that the tow line will not have any load on it while tying the knot to your boat. A knot that suddenly comes under load can have fingers in the wrong place and cause severe injury.

CHAPTER 9

EMERGENCY PROCEDURES

▶ Capsizing
▶ Heaving-To
▶ Running Aground
▶ Signaling Distress
▶ Overboard Rescue

CAPSIZING

Capsizing is one of the most dangerous aspects of sailing. The type of boat, the side of the boat on which the sails go into the water, the number of sailors on board, the wind strength, the sea conditions and the boat's position relative to the wind will be different for every capsize. Before setting out on a plan of action, it is best to analyze each situation for its unique variables before determining the best method of capsize recovery.

In any capsize, safety of the sailors is the most important consideration. Immediately after a capsize, make sure everyone is okay. Once in the water, everyone must stay with the boat. Keeping contact with the hull is important, so hold onto the boat to make sure you do not drift away.

Be aware of the fact that the boat may turn completely upside down into a turtle position. If your hull does roll over you, there may be an airspace in the cockpit where you can take a few breaths, assess the situation, and be sure no lines are wrapped around you. Then, as soon as you are able, swim out from under the boat and begin your turtled boat recovery. This airspace should only be used in an emergency situation. Please note, not all boats will have an adequate airspace. Seek advice from a certified sailing instructor who is familiar with your class of boat.

SINGLEHANDED AND DOUBLEHANDED WALKOVER (DRY) CAPSIZE RECOVERY: A *walkover capsize* in singlehanded and most doublehanded boats allows sailors to right the boat faster, avoid turtling and, less importantly, stay dry. This maneuver requires practice and good timing. A walkover capsize requires the sailor(s) to move swiftly, both as the boat capsizes and again as the boat is righted.

Follow these steps for a walkover (dry) capsize recovery:
① As the boat begins to capsize, climb over the high rail and stand on the centerboard. If you cannot perform a walkover, drop into the water quickly to prevent the boat from turtling. If you do end up in the water, make sure the mainsheet is free to run and, while maintaining contact with the boat, swim around the stern to the centerboard. Pull yourself up onto the centerboard.

② Keep your feet on the centerboard, as close to the hull as possible, to prevent damage to the tip of the centerboard. Hold onto the rail with your hands and lean back to get the boat to roll back upright. In the case of a doublehanded boat, using a jib sheet will help you lean out farther and create more leverage. Once the boat reaches the point where it will come upright without any further effort on the centerboard, prepare to scramble back into the boat.

③ Keeping your head down to avoid the swinging boom, throw your leg over the rail and slide into the boat, using your weight to balance the boat. Get control of the helm quickly and steer onto your preferred course or into the safety position until you have control of the boat.

TIP

Releasing the vang and jib sheet prior to righting the boat will reduce the likelihood of a repeat capsize.

SCOOP RECOVERY METHOD

① In the case of a doublehanded boat, if either the skipper or crew does not make it onto the high rail, they become the "scoopee". They should drop into the water and move into the scoop recovery position until the "scooper" is on the centerboard and has control of the boat to prevent it from turtling.

② Skipper and crew should check with each other to make sure everyone is safe.

③ Once either the skipper or crew is on the centerboard and ready to roll the boat upright, the other sailor should move to the middle of the cockpit just aft of the centerboard trunk, uncleat the main and jib sheets, hold onto the hiking strap, and tell the scooper he/she is ready to be scooped. It is important that the scoopee has a light grip on the hiking straps and is not pulling himself/herself up into the cockpit as the scooper begins to right the boat. A good technique is to let your life jacket keep you afloat, with your hands lightly on the hiking straps.

④ It is important for the scoopee to keep his or her head down as the boat comes back upright; the boom will have a tendency to swing across from one side of the boat to the other, either as a result of the momentum created by the boat being righted, and/or the wind's pressure on the sail.

⑤ The scoopee will also need to be prepared to use his or her weight to help balance the boat as it is righted, as well as to release any sail controls such as the vang, and main and jib sheets. If these are cleated, they might allow the sails to fill with wind and cause the boat to begin sailing.

TURTLE RECOVERY: A *turtle* occurs when the boat has turned completely upside down. Recovering from a turtle position takes longer than a scoop or singlehanded capsize; an upside-down hull is very stable and the submerged sails will resist efforts to turn the boat back upright. In some situations, the airspace in the cockpit forms a suction seal with the water, making it even harder to get the boat upright. In shallow water, a mast can get stuck in the mud, either in a complete or partially turtled position. Using the turtle recovery method will aid in righting the boat.

TIP

As part of your safety check list, it is important to make sure there is a retaining device on your daggerboard/centerboard. Without the retaining device, the daggerboard has a tendency to slip back down through the daggerboard trunk, out of the hull, and into the water where it cannot be used to right the boat.

To recover from a turtle position, the boat must be rolled upright far enough so that the masthead is at the water's surface (a capsize position). To recover, move all of your weight as far outboard on the hull as possible by standing on one of the gunnels, port or starboard, and placing your hands on the daggerboard or centerboard. Then lean outboard. On a doublehanded boat, it is often helpful for both the skipper and crew to do this together as the combined weight can be more effective. It may be a slow process to break the suction of the airspace in the hull or to ease the mast out of the mud, but be patient and keep your weight on the *gunnel* (the underside of the rail of the boat) until the boat starts to move.

Gentle bouncing can help break the suction, but if that bouncing is too pronounced you will likely break something. If your mast is stuck in the mud, be very cautious not to exert too much force trying to right the boat or you may bend the mast. In this situation, call for assistance from a safety boat.

Once you have recovered the boat into a capsize position so the masthead is at the water's surface, proceed with either a singlehanded or scoop capsize recovery. Remember, the boat may be full of water and may need to be bailed out or towed to shore before sailing again.

Patience is the biggest asset in solving a turtle capsize recovery. Righting the boat can take a long time; in some cases, it may be necessary to get outside assistance.

HEAVING-TO

Like the safety position, *heaving-to* is a method for stopping the boat to rest, eat, or listen to feedback from an instructor. Compared to the safety position, it is quieter and easier on the equipment, for the jib does not luff the way it does in the safety position. Follow these steps to heave-to:

1. Sail close to the wind with the jib sheeted in tight.
2. Tack the boat without releasing the jib or switching jib sheets.
3. Once the boat is tacked, with the jib trimmed on the windward side and fully backwinded, ease the mainsheet and the boat will slow down and come to a stop.
4. Keep the tiller to leeward, with very slight pressure in the mainsail to hold the boat at an upwind angle.

With your sails and rudder countering each other, most of the motion at this point will be slightly forward and to leeward as the boat slides sideways and downwind. Since the boat will drift to leeward (downwind), always check that there is plenty of room to drift downwind before heaving-to. To get out of a hove-to position, either release the jib and trim in on the same side as the mainsail, or pull the tiller to weather, bear off and jibe.

RUNNING AGROUND

Running aground is potentially dangerous to the boat and its sailors. Considerable damage can be done to a boat, depending on the composition of the bottom and the sea conditions. The best precaution is to know the area you are sailing in, stay away from shorelines and shallow water, and take preventive measures to avoid these areas. Running aground can usually be prevented.

TIP

If your mast is stuck in the mud...
1. As soon as your boat begins to turtle, both skipper and crew should initially get off of the boat to avoid having their weight drive the mast farther into the mud.
2. If conditions permit, try swimming the bow into the wind.

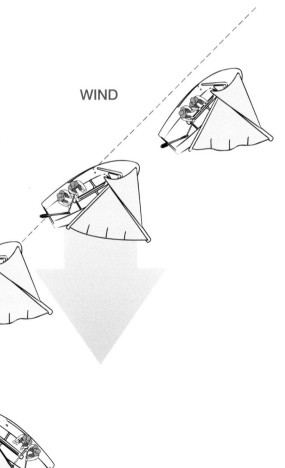

WIND

CHAPTER 9

If you run aground, safety comes first. In many situations, pulling the centerboard or daggerboard up and healing the boat will allow you to get free from a shallow area. Be aware, however, that your maneuverability will decrease with less centerboard or daggerboard in the water. Once you pull the centerboard or daggerboard up (pull the rudder up too, if it is touching bottom), if the boat does not sail or drift into deeper water, carefully gauge the depth you are in. You may be able to get out of the boat and push it back out to deeper water.

SIGNALING DISTRESS

Mishaps sometimes occur on boats that we do not plan for, and they require us to get assistance from others. For example, equipment may break or someone might get injured. Part of sailing safely and responsibly is knowing how to call for assistance when you need it.

- **Carry a whistle:** Every small-boat sailor should carry a whistle attached to their life jacket. Whistles are louder and carry further than the sound of a human voice. This can be a useful tool for attracting attention.

- **The International Signal of Distress:** One sign that boaters everywhere recognize is the International Signal of Distress. To make this signal, stretch out your arms and slowly raise them over your head until they form an "X" and then lower them again to your sides. Repeat this motion for as long as is necessary to attract attention.

OVERBOARD RESCUE

PREVENTION: Most overboard accidents can be prevented through safety awareness and by paying attention to the condition of the boat and its equipment. To prevent man overboard situations from occurring, follow the steps below:

- Check the condition of hiking straps, tiller extensions and sheets before going sailing.
- Use footwear that has grip (non-skid soles) and hold onto the boat as you move about.
- Listen to marine forecasts and watch the sky for threatening weather to avoid sudden, heavy winds that can cause accidents.

METHODS:

- **Quick-Turn Method:** In *Learn Sailing Right! Beginning Sailing,* rescuing an overboard person in water (PIW) was introduced. The hallmark of the Quick-Stop Rescue method is the immediate reduction of boat speed by turning in a direction to windward and thereafter maneuvering at modest speed, remaining near the PIW.

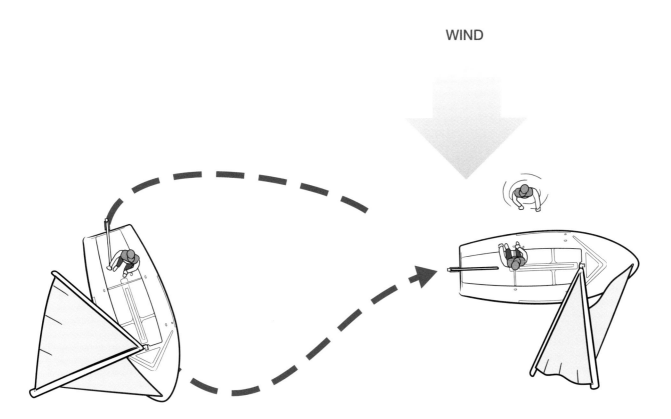

WIND

WIND

• **Heave-To Method:** Another alternative method is the Heave-To rescue method. As with the Quick-Turn method, in the Heave-To method the PIW is recovered on the windward side of the boat. Both allow for a quick return to the person in the water, which helps with communication and visibility. It is also important to constantly keep watching and talking with the person in the water and to hail "crew overboard!" loudly so other nearby vessels know there is a person in the water. The boat is tacked immediately, but the crew leaves the jib cleated. With the jib cleated, the boat runs and drifts toward the PIW. As the boat drifts downwind, the mainsail is eased fully and luffing. This method also works best in light winds.

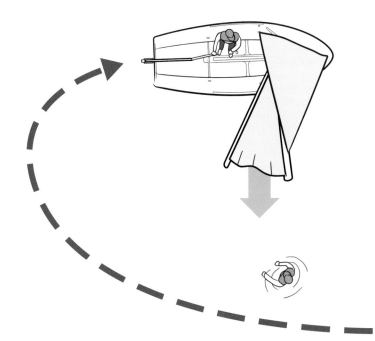

RETRIEVAL: In some instances, it may be difficult to get an overboard person back aboard. The person in the water may be exhausted, weak, or physically unable to assist themselves and you. You could also be sailing a boat with high freeboard, as is the case on large daysailers or small keelboats.

Foot loops created at the end of a line, or a line strung between two attachment points on the boat, can sometimes serve as a "step" the PIW can use when climbing back aboard.

If you are unable to get the PIW back aboard, it is important to attach them to the boat by using a line or harness around them that is knotted with a bowline and tethered to the boat. You do not want to rely on the PIW to hold onto the line for very long—particularly if he or she is tired or injured.

NAVIGATION & RULES OF THE ROAD

▶ Navigation
▶ Navigation Aids
▶ Rules of the Road

NAVIGATION

The "road map" sailors use on the water is called a *chart*. A chart identifies all the critical information mariners need to safely navigate a boat on the water including obstacles to avoid, such as shallow water and rocks, traffic channels with lane markers, and deep channels with strong currents. There are also areas where you can sail without concern for these types of obstacles. Reading a chart may take a little getting used to, but understanding the fundamentals will keep you safe. Charts also indicate the depth of the water, which is measured in feet, meters, or fathoms. When venturing out onto rivers, harbors, bays and the open ocean, it is important to understand charts and aids to navigation so you can safely reach your destination.

TIP
1 meter = 3.28 feet
1 fathom = 6 feet

NAVIGATION AIDS

Navigation aids are fixed objects, such as buoys and lighthouses, used for navigation. These markers fall into two general categories: lateral and non-lateral markers.

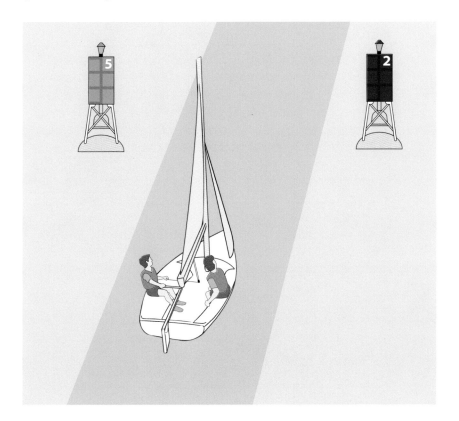

LATERAL MARKERS

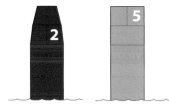

NUNS AND CANS

Red, even-numbered, cone-shaped nuns. Green, odd-numbered, cylindrical-shaped cans

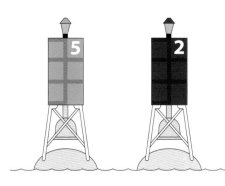

LIGHTED BUOYS
Unique flashing sequence as marked on a chart

DAYMARKS
Red triangles or green squares fixed to poles

Lateral markers are the red and green buoys or daymarks that identify the sides of channels. The area between the nuns and cans is known as a *channel.* A channel is the safe water to travel in and out of a harbor, or to navigate between obstacles. When inbound to a harbor, the red, even-numbered marks (nuns) designate the starboard side of a channel. The green, odd-numbered marks (cans) mark the port side of a channel.

Non-lateral markers are regulatory or informational markers used to advise you of situations, dangers or directions. They may indicate shoals, swim areas and speed restrictions. They can be easily identified by their orange bands on the top and bottom of each marker. Non-lateral markers are *not* used for navigation.

RULES OF THE ROAD

As a rule, less experienced sailors should try to steer clear of boating traffic. However, especially on busy waterways, interaction with other boats may be unavoidable.

On land, motorists must abide by traffic laws and the painted lanes, signs and stoplights that help prevent collisions. Similarly, boaters are obligated to respect the navigation rules, commonly referred to as the *Rules of the Road*.

As a sailor, it is your responsibility to know and understand these rules, which dictate both where boats can navigate and how to safely maneuver in traffic.

DEALING WITH TRAFFIC: Waterways can become congested with traffic. Rowboats, commercial fishing boats, recreational powerboats, ferries, cargo ships and other sailboats all share and operate in harbors and channels at the same time. To avoid potential collisions, every boater is required by law to listen and watch for other boats. This is known as *keeping a lookout.*

It is also important for all boaters to know and understand their maneuverability relative to the other boats around them. For example, if you are trying to cross a channel with a ship approaching, can you safely cross in front of that vessel? Factors in this decision include wind, current, water depth, wave height, channel width and types of boats (both your boat and the other vessel).

If you must enter a channel, keep to the edges as much as possible. If you must cross, choose a path that is perpendicular to the flow of traffic, which is the shortest distance from one side of the channel to the other. Also, be sure you are crossing at a speed/location that minimizes the chance of interfering with the paths of other boats.

NAVIGATION & RULES OF THE ROAD

WHEN TWO BOATS MEET: When sailboats cross paths, the port tack boat gives way to the starboard tack boat, the windward boat gives way to the leeward boat, and the overtaking boat gives way to the vessel ahead. If the only boats on the water were sailboats, these three simple Rules of the Road would cover just about everything you would ever need to know!

In reality, however, a busy harbor contains many different kinds of boats. Some boats are powered by sails, others by engines, and still others by oars or paddles. Some boats are light and maneuverable, while others may be large, deep-drafted and hard to turn or stop. These differences mean that some boats are less able than others to quickly alter course and avoid other boats and obstructions. Due to these variations in boat speed and maneuverability, there are navigation rules specifically addressing what to do when two different types of vessels meet. The navigation rules (also known as Col Regs) are very detailed and specific and can be cumbersome to memorize. Avoid putting yourself in a situation where the give-way rules will have to be applied. The following suggestions should help prevent a dangerous situation.

- **Sail vs. Human Power:** As a courtesy, sailboats should avoid rowboats, kayaks and canoes. Since these all use human muscle to power the oars and paddles that propel these boats through the water, they can often be slower to respond and change course.

- **Sail vs. Motor Power:** In most cases, powerboats (including sailboats under power) should give way to boats under sail. However, if the powerboat is too large to change course outside of the channel, or the powerboat cannot change course quickly enough to avoid a collision, the sailboat must give way. Powerboats with this kind of restricted maneuverability may include oil tankers, large ships, boats under tow and disabled vessels.

- **Commercial vs. Recreational:** Recreational boats, such as sailboats, should avoid commercial boats such as ferries, tour boats, cruise ships, shrimpers and trawlers.

REMEMBER, "RED RIGHT RETURNING"
Numbers increase as you return

TIP

As a general rule of courtesy, the more maneuverable boat should give way to the less maneuverable boat.

AVOID ALL COLLISIONS: Beyond knowing the rules and keeping a lookout, a good, defensive sailor should also do everything possible to *avoid all collisions.*

According to the navigation rules, in a situation when two boats must avoid one another to pass, the designated *stand-on vessel* should maintain course and speed, while the *give-way vessel* should alter course and/or speed to pass at a safe distance. In practice, however, sometimes other boaters may not necessarily know or follow the Rules of the Road. If, for whatever reason, a give-way boat is not doing its part to avoid a collision, it is much better for the stand-on vessel to alter course and avoid a collision that could potentially damage one or both boats and risk injury to someone on board. This kind of defensive sailing helps keep our waterways both fun and safe for everyone!

RESTRICTED AND/OR SAFETY ZONES: Sailors will increasingly find themselves sailing in areas, or near other vessels, that have designated *restricted* or *safety zones.* Typically these areas, if they are permanent, are marked with USCG and/or state uniform regulatory markers. Vessels, both those underway as well as those at anchor or in a berth, are usually accompanied by active marine patrol. It is every sailor's responsibility to know what zones apply to their sailing area at any given time.

MAINTENANCE

▶ Pre-Sail
▶ Post-Sail
▶ Storm Preparations

As intermediate sailors learn new skills and use more advanced equipment, more time is needed to maintain their boats and equipment. It is important to get into the routine of carefully inspecting all aspects of the boat and rigging to help insure your sail is a safe and enjoyable one. Many repairs can be accomplished by the do-it-yourself sailor, following manufacturer's guidelines.

Pre-Sail

HULL:

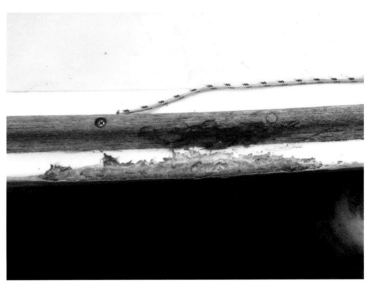

- Carefully check over the hull, deck and cockpit area of the boat. Look for chips, gouges and cracks in fiberglass boats. Water will penetrate the fiberglass in these areas and can lead to weakening and premature failure of the fiberglass. These should be filled with a waterproof marine filler appropriate for the materials used in the boat's construction, sanded smooth when cured, and covered with gelcoat or paint.
- Many new boats are also being constructed of various types of plastic. While these boats tend to be more forgiving when it comes to bumps and scrapes, different techniques are needed for making repairs. As with fiberglass repairs, check with the boat manufacturer for tips on the right materials and techniques for making a repair.
- Periodically check the underside of the hull and, in particular, the centerboard/daggerboard trunk. Many boats will have some kind of gasket secured to the opening for the centerboard. This gasket can wear out and the fittings that secure it to the boat can become loose over time.

CHAPTER 11

RIGGING AND HARDWARE:

- Inspect wire rigging for broken strands and corrosion, especially around swage fittings. A broken strand carries not just the risk of injury, but it may also be an indicator that the wire may fail. Replace any wire rigging that has broken strands.
- Check all cotter pins and split/cotter rings. Replace any that show evidence of excessive bending or stretching, and those that are not the right size for their intended use.
- Check rigging for proper tension. A loose rig can cause a loss of performance, unnecessary wear on the boat, or more serious damage to the mast partners/mast thwart.
- Check blocks, cleats and deck fittings for damage and wear. Replace any fittings that show signs of fatigue, wear to teeth or springs, or that are broken.
- Check all nuts and bolts on the boat, making sure they are properly tightened. In particular, check the rudder for excessive play in the rudder head and bracket, and the pintles and gudgeons.
- Inspect all lines and replace those that show excessive wear or chafe. Ends of lines should be whipped or melted to prevent fraying and to allow them to pass easily through blocks and fairleads.
- Check drain plugs for proper fit. Remove plugs to drain water from tanks, installing plugs after draining and before launching. Replace any that do not provide a good seal.

SAILS:

- Inspect sails for wear and tears. Sail repair tape can be a temporary repair for small holes or tears and can help prevent more substantial damage. Tape repairs, however, are a quick fix until you can return to shore and have the sail repaired properly.
- Check battens to make sure they are securely in place. A missing batten can cause premature wear to the sail. It is often a good idea to stitch or tape battens in place.

Check the condition and function of your jib and mainsail hanks, slugs and bolt ropes, as well as any sail windows.

SAFETY EQUIPMENT:

- In addition to your life jacket, there is other important safety equipment you should have. You are required to have a sound-producing device on board. A whistle (best to attach it to your life jacket) or small horn suffices as a sound-producing device.
- If your boat is not self-bailing, a bailer or bucket, sponge or pump should be included in your safety gear.
- The prudent sailor will also carry several spare clevis pins, split rings and extra lengths of line. A small multi-tool or knife and electrical tape can also be handy for making small repairs on the water, and for safety.
- Other possible gear to bring aboard includes an anchor, rode (line) and a paddle.

POST-SAIL

Refer to *Learn Sailing Right! Beginning Sailing* for a refresher on the basics of proper stowage of the boat, sails and equipment.

HULL AND RIGGING:

- Check hull and tanks for water and leaks. Water in the hull or tanks after a sail, especially if they were dry in your pre-sail inspection, indicates a problem that should be addressed.
- Remove, rinse with fresh water, and properly stow the rudder and tiller.
- Rinse the boat to remove any dirt or salt as this can lead to corrosion.
- Stow the boat properly, making sure it is tied down securely.
- Secure the boat cover, if your boat is so equipped.

SAILS AND LINES:

Remove the sails and rinse sails and lines with fresh water as necessary. If the boat turtled during your sail, make sure any traces of mud are removed—particularly at the top of the mast, in the halyard sheave box and at the top of the sail. Dirt and salt can abrade lines and sails and cause premature wear.

STORM PREPARATIONS

If there is a possibility of a storm occurring before the boat will be going out again, extra precautions should be taken. Wind in the rigging can be enough to blow the boat over. Strap the boat down securely. If the storm is expected to be severe, it may be prudent to remove the mast and rigging from the boat. A cover that does not fit securely may come loose and cause more damage; removing the cover and anything loose from the boat may be the best choice.

GLOSSARY

Apparent Wind- The altered wind direction and velocity, which is different from the true wind direction, because of the motion of the weather station.

Backstay- Is the standing rigging that runs from the top of the mast to the transom; helps pull the top of the mast aft.

Bridle- A fixed piece of line that, when shortened or lengthened, affects the boom position relative to the boat's centerline.

Center of Effort- Is the theoretical focal point of the force generated by the wind acting on the sail(s).

Center of Lateral Resistance- Is the focal point of all the forces resisting slipping sideways through the water.

Channel- The area of water between the nuns and cans.

Chart- A "road map" that sailors use on the water.

Cirrus Clouds- Wispy, and thin clouds; indicator of good weather for the day, but may be prediction that a change in weather is on the way.

Compression Battens- The battens that extend from the luff to the leech of the main.

Cumulonimbus Clouds- Towering or "thunderhead" clouds; indicator of severe conditions, including heavy rain and lightning.

Cumulus Clouds- Large, white, and fluffy clouds; indicator of good weather.

Current- The horizontal flow of water; described in terms of the direction and speed the water is moving.

Dacron- Also known as polyster lines; typically used for towing.

Ditty Bag- A small pouch where a sailor keeps tools, a knife, spare parts, a whistle, extra line, and other useful parts, pieces, and safety devices.

Draft- The depth and location of the curvature in a sail.

Drag- Is a slowing force resulting from the friction of a boat moving through the water.

Ebbing- A tide that is going out or dropping.

Fathom- A unit of length equal to six feet (1.83 meters) used especially for measuring the depth of water.

Feathering- The act of scalloping slightly towards the No-Go Zone for each puff and returning to the groove as the puff abates.

Flooding- A tide that is incoming or raising.

Footing- The act of easing sails slightly and heading down to the lower side of the groove, perhaps even into a close reach, providing more power.

Give-way Vessel- The boat that should alter course and/or speed to pass at a safe distance.

Groove- Is the course between the high and low side of close hauled, when you are making the best speed and achieving the highest pointing angle toward the wind.

Header- The wind's direction shifts from stern to bow.

Heaving-To- A method for stopping the boat to rest, eat, listen to feedback, or rest.

Hypothermia- The lowering of your core body temperature, reaching a subnormal temperature of the body.

Jib Halyard- Controls jib luff tension.

Jib Leads- Controls jib leech and foot tension.

Land Effects- Wind conditions that are affected by nearby land features such as: islands, tall buildings, or even anchored ships.

Lateral Markers- The red and green buoys or daymarks that identify the sides of channels.

Lee Helm- The boat's tendency to turn to leeward caused by too little force in the mainsail combined with too much weight on the windward side, mostly in light winds.

Lift- The wind's direction shifts from bow toward the stern.

Lull- A brief decrease in the wind.

Navigation Aids- Fixed objects, such as buoys and lighthouses, used for navigation.

Non-lateral Markers- The regulatory or informational markers used to advise you of situations, dangers, or directions.

Puff- A brief increase in the wind.

Reefing- The act of reducing the area of the mainsail by lowering the sail partially and securing the lower portion to the boom.

Rode- Another name for anchor line.

Roll Jibe- A faster paced jibe, allowing for less time with the mainsail in transition from one tack to the other while minimizing use of the rudder.

Roll Tacking- A faster-paced tack to improve acceleration once the boat has passed through the No-Go Zone.

Rules of the Road- Boats are obligated to respect the navigation rules.

Sculling- The act of moving the tiller and rudder repeatedly back and forth.

Slack- The period in between, with very little water movement.

Stand-on Vessel- The boat that should maintain course and speed.

Stratus Clouds- Low layer of clouds; indicator of steady rain.

Thermal Winds- As denser cool air is drawn toward rising warm air, wind is created. These winds are also known as "onshore breezes" or "sea breezes."

Tide- The vertical movement of water caused by the gravitational pull of the Earth and the Moon.

Traveler- A control used to adjust the location of the boom relative to the centerline of the boat and the angle of the mainsheet to the wind; usually adjusted by a car on a track at the stern of the boat.

True Wind- An accurate reading of the winds direction and velocity from a stationary point.

Turtled Boat- When a boat has capsized and turned completely upside down.

Twist- The curvature of the leech, most noticeably near the top batten.

GLOSSARY

Vang Sheeting- A technique to flatten the sail by reducing draft and minimizing power to make the boat more stable and controllable.

Walkover (Dry) Capsize- Designed for singlehanded and doublehanded boats, allowing sailors to right the boat faster, avoid turtling and, less importantly, stay dry.

Weather Helm- The boat's tendency to turn to windward caused by too much power in the mainsail, mostly in strong or puffy conditions.

Wind Shadows- Areas of less wind, usually caused by land effects or large anchored ships.

Wind Shifts- The constant changing of direction of wind.

Wind Velocity- The speed of the wind; measured in miles per hour (mph) or nautical miles per hour (knots).

Windward Heel- The tipping of a boat toward the wind due to pressure of the wind and body weight placement, especially when sailing downwind.

Anchoring	40, 44
Backstay	16, 19-20
Balance	24-29, 42, 47-48
Battens	19-21, 58
Boom vang	16-17, 19, 21, 34, 38-39
Bridle	19
Buoys	53-54
Cans	54
Capsize	38, 46
Capsize recovery	46-47
Walkover	46
Scoop	47
Turtle	48
Center of Effort	24-25
Center of Lateral Resistance	24-25
Chafe	21, 45, 58
Channel	14, 53-54
Clouds	12
Clove hitch	40-41
Collisions	540-56
C-turn jibe	35
Cunningham	16-18, 20-21, 42
Currents	14-15
Dacron	45
Daymarks	54
Distress	50
Ditty bag	7
Docking	43
Draft	16, 18-21
Drag	23-24, 33
Ebbing	14
Fathom	53
Feathering	32
Fenders	43
Flooding	14
Foils	23-24
Footing	32
Groove	31-33
Header	9
Heat	6
Heat emergencies	6
Heat exhaustion	6
Heat stroke	6
Heaving-to	49
Hiking	18, 29-30
Hydration	6
Hypothermia	6
Jib halyard	20
Jib leads	20
Knots	40-41
Land effects	13
Lateral markers	54
Lee helm	25
Lift	9, 24
Lull	8, 31-32
Mainsheet tension	17
Maintenance	57
Navigation Aids	54
No-go zone	22
Mast bend	17
Non-lateral markers	54
Nuns	54
Outhaul	17-18, 21
Overboard	50-52
Heave-to	52
Quick-turn	51
Retrieval	52
Paddling	41
Positions (skipper/crew)	26-28
Puff	8, 31-32
Pull mode	23
Push mode	22
Reefing	9, 42
Restricted zones	56
Rode	44, 58
Roll jibe	36-37
Roll tack	33
Round turn and two half-hitches	40-41
Rules of the Road	54
Rudder	22-23, 33, 35-36, 42, 49-50, 58
Running aground	49
Sail controls	16-17
Sail shape	16
Sculling	41-42
Shortening sail	42
Slack	14
Spring lines	43
Storm preparation	59
S-turn jibe	35
Tides	14
Tiller extension	30, 50
Towing	45
Traveler	19, 43, 45
Turtle	48-49, 59
Twist	16
Whistle	7, 50
Wind	8-13
Wind velocity	8
Wind reading	8
True wind	10
Apparent wind	10
Thermal wind	13
Weather	11
Weather helm	25

Notes: